THE BOOK OF BARUCH

ALSO CALLED I BARUCH

(Greek and Hebrew)

SOCIETY OF BIBLICAL LITERATURE

TEXTS AND TRANSLATIONS

PSEUDEPIGRAPHA SERIES

edited by

Robert A. Kraft

TEXTS AND TRANSLATIONS 8

PSEUDEPIGRAPHA SERIES
6

THE BOOK OF BARUCH

SCHOLARS PRESS
Missoula, Montana

THE BOOK OF BARUCH

ALSO CALLED I BARUCH

(Greek and Hebrew)

Edited, reconstructed and translated

by

EMANUEL TOV

Published by

SCHOLARS PRESS

for

The Society of Biblical Literature

Distributed by

SCHOLARS PRESS
University of Montana
Missoula, Montana 59801

THE BOOK OF BARUCH

ALSO CALLED I BARUCH

(Greek and Hebrew)

Edited, reconstructed and translated

by

EMANUEL TOV

Library of Congress Cataloging in Publication Data

Bible. O. T. Apocrypha. Baruch. Polyglot. 1975.
   The book of Baruch.

   (Pseudepigrapha series ; 6) (Society of Biblical
Literature texts and translations series ; 8)
   English, Greek, and Hebrew.
   Based on I. Tov's thesis, Hebrew University,
Jerusalem, 1973.
   Bibliography: p.
   1. Bible. O. T. Apocrypha. Baruch--Concord-
ances, Greek. 2. Bible. O. T. Apocrypha. Bar-
uch--Concordances, Hebrew. I. Tov, Imanu'el.
II. Title. III. Series: Pseudepigrapha series ;
6. IV. Series: Society of Biblical Literature.
Texts and translations ; 8.
BS1771.T68   229'.5   75-30775
ISBN 0-89130-043-0

Copyright © 1975

by

The Society of Biblical Literature

Printed in the United States of America
1 2 3 4 5
Printing Department
University of Montana
Missoula, Montana 59801

PREFACE TO THE SERIES

TEXTS AND TRANSLATIONS is a project of the Committee on Research and Publications of the Society of Biblical Literature and is under the general direction of George W. MacRae (Harvard Divinity School), Executive Secretary and Harry M. Orlinsky (Hebrew Union College-Jewish Institute of Religion, New York), Chairman of the Committee. The purpose of the project is to make available in convenient and inexpensive format ancient texts which are not easily accessible but are of importance to scholars and students of "biblical literature" as broadly defined by the Society. Reliable modern English translations will accompany the texts. Occasionally the various series will include documents not published elsewhere. It is not a primary aim of these publications to provide authoritative new critical texts, nor to furnish extensive annotations. The editions are regarded as provisional, and individual volumes may be replaced in the future as better textual evidence becomes available. The following subseries have been established thus far:

    PSEUDEPIGRAPHA, edited by Robert A. Kraft (University of Pennsylvania)

    GRECO-ROMAN RELIGION, edited by Hans Dieter Betz (School of Theology at Claremont)

    EARLY CHRISTIAN LITERATURE, edited by Birger A. Pearson (University of California at Santa Barbara)

For the PSEUDEPIGRAPHA SERIES the choice of texts is governed in part by the research interests of the SBL Pseudepigrapha Group, of which George W.E. Nickelsburg, Jr. (University of Iowa) is currently Chairman and James H. Charlesworth (Duke University) Secretary. This series will focus on Jewish materials from the Hellenistic era and will regularly include volumes that incorporate the fragmentary evidence of works attributed to biblical personalities, culled from a wide range of Jewish and Christian sources. The volumes are selected, prepared, and edited in consultation with the following editorial subcommittee of the Pseudepigrapha Group:

    Sebastian P. Brock (Oxford University, England)

    George W. MacRae (Harvard Divinity School)

    Michael E. Stone (Hebrew University, Israel)

    John Strugnell (Harvard Divinity School)

                                                  Robert A. Kraft, Editor

TABLE OF CONTENTS

INTRODUCTION

    General   1

    Reconstructing the Hebrew Vorlage of Bar 1.1-3.8   5

    The Original Language of Bar 3.9-5.9   7

    Bibliography   9

BARUCH: TEXT AND TRANSLATION   11

    Greek Text Hebrew Reconstruction (with Parallels) and English Translation of Bar 1.1-3.8

    Greek Text with English Translation of Bar 3.9-5.9

APPENDIX   37

    Greek-Hebrew Concordance to Bar 1.1-3.8   38

    Hebrew-Greek Concordance to Bar 1.1-3.8   46

INTRODUCTION[1]

The book of Baruch (Bar) has aroused much interest among scholars because of its contents, literary character, possible composite nature and its original language. As for the latter issue, Bar has been preserved in Greek, Latin, Syriac, Coptic, Ethiopic and Armenian, but there is little doubt among scholars that at least its first section (1.1-3.8) was composed in Hebrew, of which the Greek is a direct and literal translation. A tentative reconstruction of this original Hebrew text is presented here, together with the known Greek text of Bar, an English translation of the whole book, biblical parallels to the Hebrew reconstruction, and Greek-Hebrew/Hebrew-Greek concordances to Bar 1.1-3.8.[2]

(1) The G r e e k   t e x t of Bar reproduces with two minor changes J. Ziegler's reconstruction of the original form of the LXX of Bar as contained in his Ieremias, Baruch, Threni, Epistula Ieremiae, which is vol. 15 of Septuaginta: Vetus Testamentum Graecum (Göttingen: 1957). Its publisher, Vandenhoeck und Ruprecht of Göttingen, and the "Septuaginta-Kommission der Akademie der Wissenschaften zu Göttingen" (both kindly approached by Prof. R. Hanhart) permitted the use of Ziegler's text. In conformity with the general structure of the present series, the Greek text is presented here without the detailed apparatus contained in Ziegler's ed.

---

[1] The present volume has grown out of chapter 5 of the author's doctoral dissertation, The Septuagint Translation of Jeremiah and Baruch: A Discussion of an Early Revision of Jeremiah 29-52 and Baruch 1.1-3.8, written for the Hebrew University under the supervision of Professors S. Talmon and F.M. Cross, Jun. (Jerusalem, 1973). The author is grateful to his supervisors for helpful comments as well as to several others who were kind enough to make suggestions on earlier forms of the present volume: Prof. J. Strugnell and Dr. M.E. Stone commented on various facets of the reconstruction and translation, Dr. A. Hurwitz and Mr. S. Asiph on some aspects of the Hebrew, and Mrs. S. Ory corrected a few mistakes in the Greek. Thanks are due, too, to Prof. R.A. Kraft for including this booklet in the TEXTS AND TRANSLATIONS: PSEUDEPIGRAPHA SERIES and for the meticulous care with which he has guided the final stages of its preparation.

[2] The author has attempted to demonstrate in his aforementioned dissertation that initially Bar 1.1-3.8 was translated into Greek by the same translator responsible for the Greek of Jeremiah. At a second stage the translation of both works was revised towards the Hebrew. Interestingly enough, the revision has been preserved only in the "LXX" (i.e., all our old Greek MSS) of Jer 29-52 and Bar 1.1-3.8. If this hypothesis is correct, Ziegler's text represents but a second stage in the development of Bar, namely, that of the revised text.

(2) The reconstructed Hebrew original of Bar 1.1-3.8 is based on the Greek text. While the entire Hebrew reconstruction must remain tentative, a few particularly doubtful words or phrases have been noted by underlining (e.g. at 2.18). At times alternative possibilities also are suggested in parentheses (e.g. at 1.17).

The orthography of the reconstruction makes no claim to reproduce the orthography of the original Hebrew text of Bar. For better or worse, the reconstructed text follows as closely as possible the orthography of the biblical parallels to the text of Bar, which (as the whole of MT) lack a coherent and consistent pattern even though many biblical books may be characterized according to general lines of orthographic practice. Theophoric names of the type יאשיה/ יאשיהו are written in their shortened form in accordance with the custom in late Biblical times.

(3) The English translation of Bar 1.1-3.8 is made from the reconstructed original Hebrew text of Bar rather than from its Greek translation. But since the Hebrew and the Greek are, as a rule, closely related to each other in meaning, the English translation usually reflects accurately the Greek of Bar 1.1-3.8 as well. The adherence of the translation to the Hebrew reconstruction is most visible when the Greek reflects Hebrew readings that differ from the reconstruction of the original Hebrew text of Bar (see the notes at 2.9, 12.18) and when the interpretation of the Hebrew by the Greek translator differs from that preferred here. A clear example of the latter is 2.23 "streets" (חֻצוֹת) which the Greek translator interpreted wrongly, in our view, as "outside" (ἔξωθεν, cf.חוּץ).

(4) The English translation of Bar 3.9-5.9 follows the Greek text of Bar (see below on the original text of this section).

(5) Biblical parallels to the Hebrew reconstruction of Bar 1.1-3.8 (printed beneath the Hebrew text) are provided in support of the reconstruction. Such parallels, often extending to complete sentences in Bar, exist for a large proportion of the contents of Bar, especially in 1.15-2.19 (// Dan 9.5-19). The biblical parallels are of two kinds:

Parallels which probably were in the mind of the author of the Hebrew Bar and which may thus safely be taken as a basis for the reconstruction. These parallels are valid only to the degree that the Greek text can be retroverted with relative confidence into a Hebrew text which is either identical with or similar to the wording of the extant Hebrew parallel.

Biblical phrases which closely resemble the Hebrew wording conjectured to underlie the text of Bar.

INTRODUCTION

The list of parallels includes only the most important verbal parallels necessary to support the reconstruction, and excludes other parallels in both ideas and subject matter.

The Greek-Hebrew and Hebrew-Greek concordances to Bar 1.1-3.8, found in an appendix to the text of Bar, may be regarded as a modest supplement to the existing concordances to the LXX which do not list the Hebrew equivalents of words in Bar. If the LXX of Bar was produced by the same translator and reviser responsible for the LXX of Jer (see n. 2 above), many details in the text of Bar 1.1-3.8 may be as important for solving textual problems in the LXX as similar details in the LXX of Jer. These data are now accessible through the concordances provided below.

RECONSTRUCTING THE HEBREW VORLAGE OF BAR 1.1-3.8

It is, as a rule, nearly impossible to reconstruct with confidence the Hebrew Vorlage of complete sentences in the LXX, let alone of entire chapters. There are simply too many unknown factors both with regard to the translators' techniques which provide clues to any reliable reconstruction, and to the precise reconstruction of many details in the Hebrew Vorlage. I have discussed these difficulties elsewhere,[3] but have also noted that an exception may be made for reconstructing the Hebrew Vorlage of the LXX of Jer 27(34).[4] A similar exception can be made for Bar 1.1-3.8 for the following reasons:

(1) Bar has been rendered into Greek in a literal fashion by its first translator. At a later stage it was revised by someone who attempted to bring the Greek translation into greater conformity with the Hebrew text (as suggested above, n. 2). In view of the translator's (reviser's) frequent use of the usual LXX equivalents of Hebrew words, it is relatively easy to reconstrct the Hebrew Vorlage of Bar with the aid of concordances.

(2) The greater part of Bar is a mosaic of biblical passages; it quotes or elaborates upon many biblical phrases, sentences and sections which have been used to support our reconstruction.

Despite these supporting factors--without which the present reconstruction would not have been attempted--the reconstruction remains tentative. In addition to the instances of particularly doubtful retroversions which are indicated by underlining, many of the reconstructed details should be considered as mere suggestions. Thus it is impossible to know whether a certain verb has been construed with or without the nota accusativi את and whether or not the conjunctive waw has been used in a particular instance; likewise it is very hard to determine which preposition has been used in conjunction with certain verbs.

Earlier attempts to reconstruct the Hebrew Vorlage of Bar were made by J.J. Kneucker, Das Buch Baruch (Leipzig, 1879), and R.R. Harwell, The Principal Versions of Baruch (diss. Yale University, 1915). Kneucker's reconstruction is particularly helpful because it is accompanied by a very detailed commentary. Unfortunately the limited scope of the present series does not permit inclusion of extensive annotation and other support for the reconstruction beyond what is provided by the biblical parallels and the brief notes appended to the reconstruction.

---

[3] "Septuagint, the Contribution of the Septuagint to OT Research," in Interpreters' Dictionary of the Bible Supplement (forthcoming ca. 1976, Abingdon Press).

[4] "Text-critical, Literary and Exegetical Notes on the Hebrew Vorlage of the LXX of Jer. 27" (in press).

THE ORIGINAL LANGUAGE OF BAR 3.9-5.9

Unlike the above-mentioned works of Kneucker and Harwell, the present volume does not contain a reconstruction of the Hebrew Vorlage of Bar 3.9 ff. for it is not sufficiently clear that the Greek of this section was translated from Hebrew. Furthermore, even if it could be proved that at least 3.9-4.4 is based on a Hebrew text, it could not be reconstructed with the same degree of certainty as the first part of the book.

On the question of the original language, the reader is referred to Kneucker, 25 ff. and R.H. Pfeiffer, History of New Testament Times with an Introduction to the Apocrypha (Harper, 1949) 419 ff., both of whom collected impressive data suggesting that Bar 3.9-4.4 and possibly also 4.5-5.9 may have been translated from a Hebrew text. On the other hand, it should be noted that the Greek text of Bar 3.9 ff. at times seems based directly on the LXX of certain parallel passages of Jewish scripture rather than the MT.[5] This dependence could imply that Bar 3.9 ff. was originally written in Greek. Linguistic evidence indicating differences between the different sections of Bar may also point in the same direction.[6]

---

[5] The more significant examples are: Bar 3.32 = Job 28.23-24, Bar 3.33 = Job 38.34-35, Bar 4.25 = Deut 33.29, and Bar 4.29 = Zeph 3.17.

[6] The following linguistic studies have pointed out significant differences between Bar 1.1 - 3.8 and Bar 3.9 ff.: A. Wifstrand, "Die Stellung der enklitischen Personalpronomina bei den Septuaginta", Bulletin de la Societe Royale des Lettres de Lund 1949-50, 64; R.A. Martin, "Some Syntatical Criteria of Translation Greek", VT 10 (1960) 297-306, 309-310.

BIBLIOGRAPHY

For earlier selected bibliographical listings see:

    Whitehouse, O.C. "Baruch," in The Apocrypha and Pseudepigrapha of the Old Testament 1, ed. R.H. Charles (Clarendon Press, 1913) 582;

    Ward, J.M. "Baruch," in Interpreter's Dictionary of the Bible (Abingdon, 1962);

    Eissfeldt, O. The Old Testament: An Introduction (Harper & Row, 1965) 592;

    Stone, M.E. "Baruch, Book of," in Encyclopaedia Judaica (Macmillan, 1971-1972).

A more complete bibliography is contained in

    Penna, A. Baruch: La Sacra Bibbia (Turin-Rome, 1956) 18-20 and nn. 45-77.

Recent items not included in the above listings include:

    Battistone, J.J. An Examination of the Literary and Theological Background of the Wisdom Passage of the Book of Baruch (Duke University dissertation, 1968);

    Moore, Carey. "Toward the Dating of the Book of Baruch," Catholic Biblical Quarterly 36 (1974) 312-320;

    Gunneweg, A.H.J. Das Buch Baruch: Jüdische Schriften aus hellenistisch-römischer Zeit 3.2 (Gütersloh, 1975) 167-181;

    Tov, Emanuel. The Septuagint Tranlation of Jeremiah and Baruch: A Discussion of an Early Revision of Jeremiah 29-52 and Baruch 1:1-3:8 (in press, to appear 1975/76);

    Tov, Emanuel. "The Relation between the Greek Versions of Baruch and Daniel," in Armenian and Biblical Studies, ed. M.E. Stone (Armenian Patriarchate, Jerusalem, to appear 1975/76).

BARUCH

TEXT AND TRANSLATION

1.1   These are the words of the book, which Baruch the son of Neriah, the
       son of Mahseiah, the son of Zedekiah, the son Hasadiah, the son of Hilkiah,
 .2   wrote in Babylon, in the fifth year, on the seventh day of the month,
       at the time when the Chaldeans captured Jerusalem and burnt it with fire.
 .3   Baruch read the words of this book in the hearing of Jechoniah the
       son of Jehoiakim, king of Judah, and of all the people who came to (hear)
 .4   the book, the mighty men, the kings' sons, the elders, and all the
       people, from the smallest unto the greatest, all who dwelt in Babylon by
 .5-6 the river Sud. And they wept, fasted and prayed before the Lord; and
 .7   they collected money, each according to his ability, and sent it to
       Jerusalem to the priest Jehoiakim the son of Hilkiah, the son of Shallum,
       to the (other) priests and to all the people who were with him in Jeru-
 .8   salem. At that time he took the vessels of the house of the Lord,
       which had been removed from the Temple, to return them to the land of
       Judah on the tenth day of Sivan, silver vessels, which Zedekiah the son
 .9   of Josiah, king of Judah, had made after Nebuchadnezzar king of Baby-

---

1.1   Καὶ οὗτοι οἱ λόγοι τοῦ βιβλίου, οὓς ἔγραψε Βαρουχ υἱὸς
       Νηρίου υἱοῦ Μαασαίου υἱοῦ Σεδεκίου υἱοῦ Ασαδίου υἱοῦ Χελκίου
 .2   ἐν Βαβυλῶνι ἐν τῷ ἔτει τῷ πέμπτῳ ἐν ἑβδόμῃ τοῦ μηνὸς ἐν τῷ
       καιρῷ, ᾧ ἔλαβον οἱ Χαλδαῖοι τὴν Ιερουσαλημ καὶ ἐνέπρησαν αὐτὴν
       ἐν πυρί.
 .3   Καὶ ἀνέγνω Βαρουχ τοὺς λόγους τοῦ βιβλίου τούτου ἐν ὠσὶν
       Ιεχονίου υἱοῦ Ιωακιμ Βασιλέως Ιουδα καὶ ἐν ὠσὶ παντὸς τοῦ λαοῦ
 .4   τῶν ἐρχομένων πρὸς τὴν βίβλον καὶ ἐν ὠσὶ τῶν δυνατῶν καὶ υἱῶν
       τῶν βασιλέων καὶ ἐν ὠσὶ τῶν πρεσβυτέρων καὶ ἐν ὠσὶ παντὸς τοῦ
       λαοῦ ἀπὸ μικροῦ ἕως μεγάλου, πάντων τῶν κατοικούντων ἐν Βαβυλῶ-
 .5   νι ἐπὶ ποταμοῦ Σουδ. καὶ ἔκλαιον καὶ ἐνήστευον καὶ ηὔχοντο
 .6   ἐναντίον κυρίου καὶ συνήγαγον ἀργύριον, καθὰ ἑκάστου ἠδύνατο
 .7   ἡ χείρ, καὶ ἀπέστειλαν εἰς Ιερουσαλημ πρὸς Ιωακιμ υἱὸν Χελκίου
       υἱοῦ Σαλωμ τὸν ἱερέα καὶ πρὸς τοὺς ἱερεῖς καὶ πρὸς πάντα τὸν
 .8   λαὸν τοὺς εὑρεθέντας μετ' αὐτοῦ ἐν Ιερουσαλημ ἐν τῷ λαβεῖν
       αὐτὸν τὰ σκεύη οἴκου κυρίου τὰ ἐξενεχθέντα ἐκ τοῦ ναοῦ ἀπο-
       στρέψαι εἰς γῆν Ιουδα τῇ δεκάτῃ τοῦ Σιουαν, σκεύη ἀργυρᾶ, ἃ
 .9   ἐποίησε Σεδεκίας υἱὸς Ιωσία βασιλεὺς Ιουδα μετὰ τὸ ἀποικίσαι

1.1   ואלה דברי הספר אשר כתב ברוך בן נריה בן מחסיה בן צדקיה בן
2   חסדיה בן חלקיה בבבל : בשנה החמישית בשבעה לחדש בעת אשר לכדו
       הכשדים את ירושלם וישרפוה באש :
3   ויקרא ברוך את דברי הספר הזה באזני יכניה בן יהויקים מלך יהודה
4   ובאזני כל העם הבאים אל הספר : ובאזני הגברים ובני המלכים ובאזני
       הזקנים ובאזני כל העם (ל)מקטן (ו)עד גדול כל הישבים בבבל על נהר
5-6   סוד : ויבכו ויצומו ויתפללו לפני ה' : ויקבצו כסף __איש כאשר השיגה__
7   __ידו__ : וישלחו ירושלם אל יהויקים בן חלקיה בן שלום הכהן ואל הכהנים
8   ואל כל העם הנמצאים עמו בירושלם : בקחתו את כלי בית ה' המוצאים מן
       ההיכל להשיב אל ארץ יהודה בעשרה לסיון כלי כסף אשר עשה צדקיה בן
9   יאשיה מלך יהודה : אחרי הגלות נבוכדנאצר מלך בבל את יכניה ואת

1	ואלה דברי הספר אשר שלח ירמיה	Jer 29.1
	ברוך בן נריה בן מחסיה	Jer 32.12
2	ולכדוה ושרפה באש	Jer 34.22
3	ויקרא באזניהם את כל דברי ספר הברית	2 Kgs 23.2
	וקראת...באזני כל יהודה הבאים	Jer 36.6
4	וכל העם למקטן ועד גדול	2 Kgs 23.2
5	ויבכו...ויצומו	Judg 20.26
	ויתפלל...לפני ה'	2 Kgs 19.15
6	וקבצו...כסף	2 Chr 24.5
	על פי אשר תשיג יד הנדר	Lev 27.8
7	העם הנמצאים עמו	1 Sam 13.15
8	להשיב כלי בית ה' וכל הגולה מבבל אל המקום הזה	Jer 28.6
	כלי בית ה' מושבים מבבלה	Jer 27.16
	ויוצא...כלי הזהב אשר עשה שלמה...	2 Kgs 24.13
	ואף מאני בית אלהא די דהבא וכספא די נבוכדנצר הנפק מן היכלא די בירושלם והיבל לבבל יהתיבון ויהך להיכלא די בירושלם לאתרה ותחת בבית אלהא	Ezra 6.5
9	אחרי הגלות נבוכדנאצר מלך בבל את יכניהו בן יהויקים מלך יהוה ואת שרי יהודה ואת החרש ואת המסגר מירושלם ויבאם בבל	Jer 24.1

BARUCH

lon, had exiled Jechoniah, the rulers, the smiths, the mighty men and the people of rank from Jerusalem, and had brought them to Babylon.

.10 They said: "Behold, we are sending you money; so buy with the money burnt offerings, sin offerings and incense, prepare cereal offerings and offer
.11 (them) upon the altar of the Lord our God. Pray for the life of Nebuchadnezzar king of Babylon and of his son Belshazzar, that their days may endure as the
.12 days of the heaven above the earth. And pray that the Lord will give us strength and will lighten our eyes, that we shall live under the protection of Nebuchadnezzar king of Babylon and of his son Belshazzar, and that we shall
.13 find favor in their sight. Also pray for us to the Lord our God, for we have sinned against the Lord our God and the wrath and anger of the Lord have not
.14 turned from us until this day. Lastly, read this book which we are sending you and make confession in the house of the Lord on the day of the feast and during the days of the solemn assembly.
.15 You shall say: "To the Lord our God belongs righteousness, but confusion

---

Ναβουχοδονοσορ βασιλέα Βαβυλῶνος τὸν Ιεχονίαν καὶ τοὺς ἄρχοντας καὶ τοὺς δεσμώτας καὶ τοὺς δυνατοὺς καὶ τὸν λαὸν τῆς γῆς ἀπὸ Ιερουσαλημ καὶ ἤγαγεν αὐτοὺς^a εἰς Βαβυλῶνα.

.10 Καὶ εἶπαν Ἰδοὺ ἀπεστείλαμεν πρὸς ὑμᾶς ἀργύριον, καὶ ἀγοράσατε τοῦ ἀργυρίου ὁλοκαυτώματα καὶ περὶ ἁμαρτίας καὶ λίβανον καὶ ποιήσατε μαναα καὶ ἀνοίσατε ἐπὶ τὸ θυσιαστήριον κυρίου θεοῦ
.11 ἡμῶν καὶ προσεύξασθε περὶ τῆς ζωῆς Ναβουχοδονοσορ βασιλέως Βαβυλῶνος καὶ εἰς ζωὴν Βαλτασαρ υἱοῦ αὐτοῦ, ἵνα ὦσιν αἱ ἡμέραι
.12 αὐτῶν ὡς αἱ ἡμέραι τοῦ οὐρανοῦ ἐπὶ τῆς γῆς. καὶ δώσει κύριος ἰσχὺν ἡμῖν καὶ φωτίσει τοὺς ὀφθαλμοὺς ἡμῶν, καὶ ζησόμεθα ὑπὸ τὴν σκιὰν Ναβουχοδονοσορ βασιλέως Βαβυλῶνος καὶ ὑπὸ τὴν σκιὰν Βαλτασαρ υἱοῦ αὐτοῦ καὶ δουλεύσομεν αὐτοῖς ἡμέρας πολλὰς καὶ
.13 εὑρήσομεν χάριν ἐναντίον αὐτῶν. καὶ προσεύξασθε περὶ ἡμῶν πρὸς κύριον θεὸν ἡμῶν, ὅτι ἡμάρτομεν τῷ κυρίῳ θεῷ ἡμῶν, καὶ οὐκ ἀπέστρεψεν ὁ θυμὸς κυρίου καὶ ἡ ὀργὴ αὐτοῦ ἀφ'ἡμῶν ἕως τῆς
.14 ἡμέρας ταύτης. καὶ ἀναγνώσεσθε τὸ βιβλίον τοῦτο, ὃ ἀπεστείλαμεν πρὸς ὑμᾶς ἐξαγορεῦσαι ἐν οἴκῳ κυρίου ἐν ἡμέρᾳ ἑορτῆς καὶ ἐν ἡμέραις καιροῦ.
.15 Καὶ ἐρεῖτε Τῷ κυρίῳ θεῷ ἡμῶν ἡ δικαιοσύνη, ἡμῖν δὲ αἰσχύνη

1.10-15

השרים ואת המסגר ואת הגברים ואת עם הארץ מירושלם ויבאם^a בבל :

10 ויאמרו הנה שלחנו אליכם כסף וקנו בכסף עולות וחטאת ולבונה

11 ועשו מנחה והעלו על מזבח ה׳ אלהינו : והתפללו בעד חיי נבוכדנאצר מלך בבל ובעד (ואל) חיי בלשאצר בנו למען יהיו ימיהם כימי השמים על

12 הארץ : ויתן ה׳ עז לנו ויאר את עינינו ונחי(ה) בצל נבוכדנאצר מלך בבל ובצל בלשאצר בנו ונעבד אתם ימים רבים ונמצא חן בעיניהם :

13 והתפללו בעדנו אל ה׳ אלהינו כי חטאנו לה׳ אלהינו ולא שב אף ה׳

14 וחמתו ממנו עד היום הזה : וקראו את הספר הזה אשר שלחנו אליכם להתודות בבית ה׳ ביום חג ובימי מועד :

15 ואמרו לה׳ אלהינו הצדקה ולנו בשת הפנים כיום הזה לאיש יהודה

---

10 מבאים עולה וזבח ומנחה ולבונה	Jer 17.26
11 למען ירבו ימיכם ... כימי השמים על הארץ	Deut 11.21
התפלל נא בעדנו אל ה׳	Jer 37.3
די להון מהקרבין ניחוחין לאלה שמיא ומצלין לחיי מלכא ובנוהי	Ezra 6.10
12 ה׳ עז לעמו יתן	Ps 29.11
האירה עיני	Ps 13.4
ובצלו ישבו כל גוים רבים	Ezek 31.6
לא תעבדו את מלך בבל	Jer 27.9
13 ישב נא אפך וחמתך מעירך ירושלם	Dan 9.16
14 ויקראו בספר תורת ה׳ ... מתודים ומשתחוים לה׳ אלהיהם	Neh 9.3
מה תעשו ליום מועד וליום חג ה׳	Hos 9.5
15 לך ה׳ הצדקה ולנו בשת הפנים כיום הזה לאיש יהודה ולישבי ירושלם	Dan 9.7

---

^{a} Based on αὐτούς which is found in the majority of the MSS. A few MSS (among which codex B) read αὐτόν (thus also Ziegler's edition of Bar).

	of face, now as ever, belongs to us, the men of Judah and the inhabi-
.16	tants of Jerusalem, and to our kings, rulers, priests, prophets and
.17-8	ancestors; for we have sinned against the Lord; we have disobeyed
	him and we have not listened to the voice of the Lord our God telling
.19	us to follow the law(s)[b] which he has set before us. From the day when
	the Lord brought our forefathers out of the land of Egypt to this day we
.20	have defied the Lord our God and we have refused to obey him. Therefore
	the evil and the curse which the Lord commanded through his servant Moses
	on the day that he brought our forefathers out of the land of Egypt to give
	us a land flowing with milk and honey, that evil and curse have clung
.21	to us, as they still do today. We have been disobedient to the Lord our
	God by not listening to all the words of the prophets whom he has sent to
.22	us, but we walked each in the stubbornness of his own evil heart by
	serving other gods and by doing what is evil in the sight of the Lord our
	God.
2.1	Therefore the Lord carried out the threat which he had spoken
	against us, against our Judges who judged Israel, our kings and rulers and

---

τῶν προσώπων ὡς ἡ ἡμέρα αὕτη, ἀνθρώπῳ Ιουδα καὶ τοῖς κατοι-
.16 κοῦσιν Ιερουσαλημ   καὶ τοῖς βασιλεῦσιν ἡμῶν καὶ τοῖς ἄρχουσιν
ἡμῶν καὶ τοῖς ἱερεῦσιν ἡμῶν καὶ τοῖς προφήταις ἡμῶν καὶ τοῖς
.17-8 πατράσιν ἡμῶν, ὧν ἡμάρτομεν ἐναντίον κυρίου   καὶ ἠπειθήσαμεν
αὐτῷ καὶ οὐκ ἠκούσαμεν τῆς φωνῆς κυρίου θεοῦ ἡμῶν πορεύεσθαι
.19 τοῖς προστάγμασι κυρίου, οἷς ἔδωκε κατὰ πρόσωπον ἡμῶν.   ἀπὸ
τῆς ἡμέρας, ἧς ἐξήγαγε κύριος τοὺς πατέρας ἡμῶν ἐκ γῆς Αἰγύπτου,
καὶ ἕως τῆς ἡμέρας ταύτης ἤμεθα ἀπειθοῦντες πρὸς κύριον θεὸν
.20 ἡμῶν καὶ ἐσχεδιάζομεν πρὸς τὸ μὴ ἀκούειν τῆς φωνῆς αὐτοῦ.   καὶ
ἐκολλήθη εἰς ἡμᾶς τὰ κακὰ καὶ ἡ ἀρά, ἣν συνέταξε κύριος τῷ
Μωυσῇ παιδὶ αὐτοῦ ἐν ἡμέρᾳ, ᾗ ἐξήγαγε τοὺς πατέρας ἡμῶν ἐκ γῆς
Αἰγύπτου δοῦναι ἡμῖν γῆν ῥέουσαν γάλα καὶ μέλι ὡς ἡ ἡμέρα αὕτη.
.21 καὶ   οὐκ ἠκούσαμεν τῆς φωνῆς κυρίου θεοῦ ἡμῶν κατὰ πάντας τοὺς
.22 λόγους τῶν προφητῶν, ὧν ἀπέστειλε πρὸς ἡμᾶς,   καὶ ᾠχόμεθα ἕκαστος ἐν διανοίᾳ καρδίας αὐτοῦ τῆς πονηρᾶς ἐργάζεσθαι θεοῖς ἑτέ-
ροις ποιῆσαι τὰ κακὰ κατ'ὀφθαλμοὺς κυρίου θεοῦ ἡμῶν.
2.1   Καὶ ἔστησε κύριος τὸν λόγον αὐτοῦ, ὃν ἐλάλησεν ἐφ'ἡμᾶς καὶ
ἐπὶ τοὺς δικαστὰς ἡμῶν τοὺς δικάσαντας τὸν Ισραηλ καὶ ἐπὶ τοὺς

1.16-2.1

16 ולישבי ירושלם : ולמלכינו ולשרינו ולכהנינו ולנביאינו ולאבותינו :

17-18 אשר חטאנו לה׳ (לפני ה׳) : ומרדנו בו ולא שמענו בקול ה׳ אלהינו

19 ללכת בתורת ^{b} ה׳ אשר נתן לפנינו : (ל)מן היום אשר הוציא ה׳ את
אבותינו מארץ מצרים ועד היום הזה ממרים היינו עם ה׳ אלהינו וסור

20 לבלתי שמוע בקולו : ותדבק בנו הרעה והאלה אשר צוה ה׳ למשה עבדו
ביום הוציא את אבותינו מארץ מצרים לתת לנו ארץ זבת חלב ודבש כיום

21 הזה : ולא שמענו בקול ה׳ אלהינו ככל דברי הנבאים אשר שלח אלינו :

22 ונלך איש בשררות לבו הרע לעבוד אלהים אחרים לעשות את הרע בעיני ה׳
אלהינו :

2.1 ויקם ה׳ את דברו אשר דבר עלינו ועל שפטינו השפטים את ישראל

7-16 ולמלכינו לשרינו ולאבתינו אשר חטאנו לך	Dan 9.8
למלכינו לשרינו ולכהנינו ולנביאינו ולאבתינו ... :	Neh 9.32-33
ואנחנו הרשענו	
18 ולא שמענו בקול ה׳ אלהינו ללכת בתורתיו אשר נתן לפנינו	Dan 9.10
וימרו וימרדו בך וישלכו את תורתך אחרי גום	Neh 9.26
19 למן היום אשר יצאת מארץ מצרים עד ... ממרים הייתם עם ה׳	Deut 9.7
למן היום אשר יצאו אבותיכם מארץ מצרים עד היום הזה	Jer 7.25
וסור לבלתי שמוע בקלך	Dan 9.11
20 ותתך עלינו האלה והשבעה אשר כתובה בתורת משה עבד האלהים	Dan 9.11
ורבצה ^{c} בו כל האלה	Deut 29.19
ידבקו בו כול אלות הברית הזות	1 Q S 2.16
אשר צויתי את אבותיכם ביום הוציאי אותם מארץ מצרים ... : לתת להם ארץ זבת חלב ודבש כיום הזה	Jer 11.4-5
21-2 ולא שמעו ... וילכו במעצות בשררות לבם הרע	Jer 7.24
21 לשמע על דברי עבדי הנבאים אשר אנכי שלח אליכם	Jer 26.5
22 אך עשים הרע בעיני	Jer 32.30
1 ויקם את דבריו(דברו : Q) אשר דבר עלינו ועל שפטינו אשר שפטונו	Dan 9.12

---

^{b} The LXX reflects a noun in the plural both here and in 2.10 (thus also Dan 9.10 MT and Th.). Possibly the original text contained in all three verses a noun in the singular which was understood incorrectly as a defectively written plural noun. The singular noun has been preserved in the LXX translation of Dan 9.10.

^{c} LXX: κολλάομαι as in Bar 1.20.

.2 the men of Israel and Judah. It has never happened under heaven as it
happened in Jerusalem, in conformity with what is written in the Law of
.3 Moses, that we would eat the flesh of our own sons and daughters.
.4 Furthermore, he has made them repugnant to all the kingdoms that are
around us, as an object of reproach and horror among all the nations
.5 around us to which the Lord has banished them. Therefore they were
downcast rather than uplifted, because we had sinned against the Lord
our God by not obeying him.
.6   To the Lord our God belongs righteousness, but confusion of face,
.7 now as ever, belongs to us and our ancestors. The things which God has
.8 said about us, all this evil has come upon us. Yet we have not tried
to win the favor of the Lord by turning, each of us, from the thoughts
.9 of his wicked heart. Therefore the Lord kept watch on the evil and
he brought it upon us, for the Lord is righteous in all his deeds (with
.10 regard to the things) which he has commanded us. Yet we have not
listened to his voice telling us to follow the law(s) which he set
before us.

βασιλεῖς ἡμῶν καὶ ἐπὶ τοὺς ἄρχοντας ἡμῶν καὶ ἐπὶ ἄνθρωπον Ισραηλ
.2 καὶ Ιουδα.   οὐκ ἐποιήθη ὑποκάτω παντὸς τοῦ οὐρανοῦ καθὰ ἐποίη-
.3 σεν ἐν Ιερουσαλημ κατὰ τὰ γεγραμμένα ἐν τῷ νόμῳ Μωυσῆ   τοῦ
φαγεῖν ἡμᾶς ἄνθρωπον σάρκας υἱοῦ αὐτοῦ καὶ ἄνθρωπον σάρκας
.4 θυγατρὸς αὐτοῦ.   καὶ ἔδωκεν αὐτοὺς ὑποχειρίους πάσαις ταῖς
βασιλείαις ταῖς κύκλῳ ἡμῶν εἰς ὀνειδισμὸν καὶ εἰς ἄβατον ἐν
πᾶσι τοῖς λαοῖς τοῖς κύκλῳ ἡμῶν, οὗ διέσπειρεν αὐτοὺς κύριος
.5 ἐκεῖ.   καὶ ἐγενήθησαν ὑποκάτω καὶ οὐκ ἐπάνω, ὅτι ἡμάρτομεν τῷ
κυρίῳ θεῷ ἡμῶν πρὸς τὸ μὴ ἀκούειν τῆς φωνῆς αὐτοῦ.
.6   Τῷ κυρίῳ θεῷ ἡμῶν ἡ δικαιοσύνη, ἡμῖν δὲ καὶ τοῖς πατράσιν
.7 ἡμῶν ἡ αἰσχύνη τῶν προσώπων ὡς ἡ ἡμέρα αὕτη. ἃ ἐλάλησε κύριος
.8 ἐφ'ἡμᾶς, πάντα τὰ κακὰ ταῦτα ἦλθεν ἐφ'ἡμᾶς. καὶ οὐκ ἐδεήθημεν
τοῦ προσώπου κυρίου τοῦ ἀποστρέψαι ἕκαστον ἀπὸ τῶν νοημάτων τῆς
.9 καρδίας αὐτῶν τῆς πονηρᾶς. καὶ ἐγρηγόρησε κύριος ἐπὶ τοῖς
κακοῖς, καὶ ἐπήγαγε κύριος ἐφ'ἡμᾶς, ὅτι δίκαιος ὁ κύριος ἐπὶ
.10 πάντα τὰ ἔργα αὐτοῦ, ἃ ἐνετείλατο ἡμῖν. καὶ οὐκ ἠκούσαμεν τῆς
φωνῆς αὐτοῦ πορεύεσθαι τοῖς προστάγμασι κυρίου, οἷς ἔδωκε κατὰ
πρόσωπον ἡμῶν.

2.2-10

2   ועל מלכינו ועל שרינו ועל איש ישראל ויהודה : לא נעשתה תחת כל
3   השמים כאשר <u>נעשתה</u> בירושלם ככתוב בתורת משה : לאכל איש (את) בשר
4   בנו ואיש (את) בשר בתו : ויתן אתם לזועה (לזעוה) לכל הממלכות אשר
    סביבתינו לחרפה ולשמה בכל הגוים (אשר) סביבתינו אשר הדיחם ה' שם :
5   ויהיו למטה ולא למעלה כי חטאנו לה' אלהינו לבלתי שמע בקולו :
6-7 לה' אלהינו הצדקה ולנו ולאבותינו בשת הפנים כיום הזה : אשר
8   דבר ה' עלינו כל הרעה הזאת באה עלינו : ולא חלינו את פני ה' לשוב
9   איש ממחשבות (ממועצות) לבם הרע : וישקד ה' על הרעה ויביאה^d עלינו
10 כי צדיק ה' על כל מעשיו אשר צוה אתנו (לנו) : ולא שמענו בקולו
    ללכת בתורת^e ה' אשר נתן לפנינו :

Dan 9.12-13	2 להביא עלינו רעה גדלה אשר לא נעשתה תחת כל השמים כאשר
	נעשתה בירושלם : כאשר כתוב בתורת משה
Jer 19.9	3 והאכלתים את בשר בניהם ואת בשר בנתיהם ואיש בשר רעהו
	יאכלו
Lev 26.29	ואכלתם בשר בניכם ובשר בנתיכם תאכלו
Jer 29.18	4 ונתתים לזועה (לזעוה : Q) לכל ממלכות הארץ לאלה
	ולשמה ולשרקה ולחרפה בכל הגוים אשר הדחתים שם
Deut 28.13	5 והיית רק למעלה ולא תהיה למטה
Dan 9.8	אשר חטאנו לך
Dan 9.11	לבלתי שמע בקלך
Dan 9.7	6 לך אדני הצדקה ולנו בשת הפנים כיום הזה
Dan 9.12	7 אשר דבר עלינו
Dan 9.13	כל הרעה הזאת באה עלינו
Dan 9.13	8 ולא חלינו את פני ה' אלהינו לשוב מעוננו
Jer 7.24	וילכו במעצות בשררות לבם הרע
Dan 9.14	9 וישקד ה' על הרעה ויביאה עלינו כי צדיק ה' אלהינו על
	כל מעשיו אשר עשה
Dan 9.10	10 ולא שמענו בקול ה' אלהינו ללכת בתורתיו אשר נתן לפנינו

---

^{d} Emended from ריבֿ(י)א הי' reflected by the LXX; cf. also the parallel passage Dan 9.14.

^{e} See note b, above.

.11   And now, O Lord, God of Israel, who brought your people out of
the land of Egypt with a mighty hand, with signs and portents, with
great power and with an outstretched arm, making for yourself a name
.12 which lives on to this day, we have sinned, we have done wrong and we
.13 have acted wickedly. O Lord our God, we beg that by all your deeds
of justice your wrath may depart from us, for we are left as a few
.14 among the nations to which you have banished us. Listen, O Lord, to
our prayer and supplication and deliver us for your own sake and grant
.15 us favor with our captors, so that the whole world may know that you
are the Lord our God, for Israel and his people are called by your
.16 name. O Lord, look down from your holy dwelling place and consider us,
.17 incline your ear, O Lord, and hear; open your eyes and see, for not
the dead who are in their graves, whose spirits have been removed from
their bodies, will give honor to the Lord and will praise his justice,
.18 but a trembling heart and a foot which walks while bent and feeble,
failing eyes and a languishing soul will give you honor and praise your
justice, O Lord.

.11   Καὶ νῦν, κύριε ὁ θεὸς Ισραηλ, ὃς ἐξήγαγες τὸν λαόν σου ἐκ
γῆς Αἰγύπτου ἐν χειρὶ κραταιᾷ καὶ ἐν σημείοις καὶ ἐν τέρασι καὶ
ἐν δυνάμει μεγάλῃ καὶ ἐν βραχίονι ὑψηλῷ καὶ ἐποίησας σεαυτῷ ὄνο-
.12 μα ὡς ἡ ἡμέρα αὕτη,   ἡμάρτομεν, ἠσεβήσαμεν ἠδικήσαμεν, κύριε ὁ
.13 θεὸς ἡμῶν, ἐπὶ πᾶσι τοῖς δικαιώμασί σου.   ἀποστραφήτω ὁ θυμός
σου ἀφ' ἡμῶν, ὅτι κατελείφθημεν ὀλίγοι ἐν τοῖς ἔθνεσιν, οὗ διέ-
.14 σπειρας ἡμᾶς ἐκεῖ.   εἰσάκουσον, κύριε, τῆς προσευχῆς ἡμῶν καὶ
τῆς δεήσεως ἡμῶν καὶ ἐξελοῦ ἡμᾶς ἕνεκεν σοῦ καὶ δὸς ἡμῖν χάριν
.15 κατὰ πρόσωπον τῶν ἀποικισάντων ἡμᾶς,   ἵνα γνῷ πᾶσα ἡ γῆ ὅτι σὺ
κύριος ὁ θεὸς ἡμῶν, ὅτι τὸ ὄνομά σου ἐπεκλήθη ἐπὶ Ισραηλ καὶ ἐπὶ
.16 τὸ γένος αὐτοῦ.   κύριε, κάτιδε ἐκ τοῦ οἴκου τοῦ ἁγίου σου καὶ
.17 ἐννόησον εἰς ἡμᾶς· κλῖνον, κύριε, τὸ οὖς σου καὶ ἄκουσον· ἄν-
οιξον ὀφθαλμούς σου καὶ ἴδε· ὅτι οὐχ οἱ τεθνηκότες ἐν τῷ ᾅδῃ,
ὧν ἐλήμφθη τὸ πνεῦμα αὐτῶν ἀπὸ τῶν σπλάγχνων αὐτῶν, δώσουσι
.18 δόξαν καὶ δικαίωμα τῷ κυρίῳ, ἀλλὰ ἡ ψυχὴ ἡ λυπουμένη ἐπὶ τὸ
μέγεθος, ὃ βαδίζει κύπτον καὶ ἀσθενοῦν καὶ οἱ ὀφθαλμοὶ οἱ ἐκ-
λείποντες καὶ ἡ ψυχὴ ἡ πεινῶσα δώσουσί σοι δόξαν καὶ δικαιοσύ-
νην, κύριε.

11 ועתה ה׳ אלהי ישראל אשר הוצאת את עמך מארץ מצרים ביד חזקה
    ובאתות ובמופתים (ו)בכח גדול ובזרע נטויה ותעש לך שם כיום הזה:
12-13 חטאנו (ה)(ע)וינו (ה)רשענו: ה׳ אלהינו ככל צדקתיך ישב אפך ממנו כי
14 נשארנו מעט בגוים אשר הדחתנו שם: שמע ה׳ אל תפלתנו ואל תחנונינו
15 והצילנו למענך ותן לנו חן לפני שובינו: למען תדע כל הארץ כי אתה
16 ה׳ אלהינו כי שמך נקרא על ישראל ועל עמו: ה׳ השקיפה ממעון קדשך
17 ושים לבך (והבט) אלינו הטה ה׳ אזנך ושמע: פקח עיניך וראה כי לא
18 המתים בשאול אשר לקחה רוחם מקרבם יתנו כבוד וצדקה לה׳: כי לב
    רגז ורגל^g ההלכת כפופה ו(נ)כשלה וכליון עינים ודאבון^h נפש יתנו לך
    כבוד וצדקה ה׳:

Dan 9.15	11 ועתה אדני אלהינו אשר הוצאת את עמך מארץ מצרים ביד
	חזקה ותעש לך שם כיום הזה
Jer 32.21	ותצא את עמך את ישראל מארץ מצרים באתות ובמופתים וביד
	חזקה ובאזרוע נטויה
Dan 9.5	12 חטאנו ועוינו והרשענו
1 Kgs 8.47	חטאנו והעוינו רשענו
2 Chr 6.37	חטאנו העוינו ורשענו
Dan 9.16	אדני ככל צדקתך ישב נא אפך וחמתך מעירך
Jer 42.3	13 כי נשארנו מעט מהרבה
Dan 9.17	14 ועתה שמע אלהינו אל תפלת עבדך ואל תחנוניו ... למען ה׳
Gen 39.21	ויתן חנו בעיני שר בית הסהר
2 Kgs 19.19	15 הושיענו נא מי־דו וידעו כל ממלכות הארץ כי אתה ה׳
	אלהים לבדך
Dan 9.19	כי שמך נקרא על עירך ועל עמך
Deut 26.15	16 השקיפה ממעון קדשך מן השמים
Dan 9.18	הטה אלהי אזנך ושמע פקח עיניך וראה שממתינו
Isa 38.18	17 כי לא שאול תודך מות יהללך
Ps 6.6	כי אין במות זכרך בשאול מי יודה לך
Deut 28.65	18 לב רגז וכליון עינים ודאבון נפש

---

^{f} The Hebrew and Greek sentence divisions differ because δικαίωμα is contextually very awkward in the Greek. Moreover, the sequence in Dan 9.16 may be used to rearrange the text of Bar since the whole of Bar 1.15-2.19 is based on Dan 9.5-19. While the original text of Bar presumably had ככל, the Greek translator may have found על כל, or made a contextual adaptation in his translation.

^{g} Emended from ורהגדל reflected by the LXX.

^{h} πεινάω seemingly reflects רעב as elsewhere in the LXX. However, both here and in Jer 31(38).12,25 the translator's Vorlage apparently contained the

.19 For not by virtue of the righteous deeds of our ancestors and kings
.20 do we present our supplication before you, O Lord our God. For you
sent your wrath and anger upon us, as you spoke through your servants
.21 the prophets, saying: "Thus says the Lord: Bow your shoulders and
serve the king of Babylon and you will dwell in the land which I gave
.22 to your forefathers. But if you will not obey the Lord by refusing to
.23 serve the king of Babylon, I will banish from the cities of Judah
and from the streets of Jerusalem the sounds of joy and gladness, the
voice of bridegroom and bride, and the whole land shall be desolate
without inhabitants.
.24 But we did not obey your command to serve the king of Babylon and
therefore you carried out the threat which you spoke through your servants the prophets, namely to bring out the bones of our kings and
.25 fathers from their resting places, and they are now exposed to heat
by day and frost by night. And people died with bad diseases (by bad
.26 plagues), by famine, sword and pestilence. Furthermore, you made the
house which is called by your name desolate, as it still is today, because

---

.19 Ὅτι οὐκ ἐπὶ τὰ δικαιώματα τῶν πατέρων ἡμῶν καὶ τῶν βασιλέων
ἡμῶν ἡμεῖς καταβάλλομεν τὸν ἔλεον ἡμῶν κατὰ πρόσωπόν σου, κύριε
.20 ὁ θεὸς ἡμῶν,   ὅτι ἐνῆκας τὸν θυμόν σου καὶ τὴν ὀργήν σου εἰς
ἡμᾶς, καθάπερ ἐλάλησας ἐν χειρὶ τῶν παίδων σου τῶν προφητῶν
.21 λέγων   Οὕτως εἶπε κύριος   Κλίνατε τὸν ὦμον ὑμῶν καὶ ἐργάσασθε
τῷ βασιλεῖ Βαβυλῶνος καὶ καθίσατε ἐπὶ τὴν γῆν, ἣν ἔδωκα τοῖς
.22 πατράσιν ὑμῶν· καὶ ἐὰν μὴ ἀκούσητε τῆς φωνῆς κυρίου ἐργάσασθαι
.23 τῷ βασιλεῖ Βαβυλῶνος,   ἐκλείψειν ποιήσω ἐκ πόλεων Ιουδα καὶ
ἔξωθεν Ιερουσαλημ φωνὴν εὐφροσύνης καὶ φωνὴν χαρμοσύνης, φωνὴν
νυμφίου καὶ φωνὴν νύμφης, καὶ ἔσται πᾶσα ἡ γῆ εἰς ἄβατον ἀπὸ
ἐνοικούντων.
.24 Καὶ οὐκ ἠκούσαμεν τῆς φωνῆς σου ἐργάσασθαι τῷ βασιλεῖ Βαβυλῶνος, καὶ ἔστησας τοὺς λόγους σου, οὓς ἐλάλησας ἐν χερσὶ τῶν
παίδων σου τῶν προφητῶν τοῦ ἐξενεχθῆναι τὰ ὀστᾶ βασιλέων ἡμῶν
.25 καὶ τὰ ὀστᾶ τῶν πατέρων ἡμῶν ἐκ τοῦ τόπου αὐτῶν,   καὶ ἰδοὺ
ἐστιν ἐξερριμμένα τῷ καύματι τῆς ἡμέρας καὶ τῷ παγετῷ τῆς νυκτός,
καὶ ἀπεθάνοσαν ἐν πόνοις πονηροῖς, ἐν λιμῷ καὶ ἐν ῥομφαίᾳ καὶ ἐν
.26 ἀποστολῇ. καὶ ἔθηκας τὸν οἶκον, οὗ ἐπεκλήθη τὸ ὄνομά σου ἐπ' αὐτῷ,

2.19-26

19   כי לא על צדקות אבותינו ומלכינו אנחנו מפילים תחנונינו לפניך
20   ה׳ אלהינו : כי שלחת אפך וחמתך בנו כאשר דברת ביד עבדיך הנבאים
21   לאמר : כה אמר ה׳ הטו צואריכם ועבדו את מלך בבל ושבו על הארץ אשר
22-23 נתתי לאבותיכם : ואם לא תשמעו בקול ה׳ לעבד את מלך בבל : (ו)השבתי
      מערי יהודה ומחצות‏^{i}ירושלם קול ששון וקול שמחה קול חתן וקול כלה
      והיתה כל הארץ לשמה מאין יושב :
24   ולא שמענו בקולך לעבד את מלך בבל ותקם את דבריך אשר דברת ביד
      עבדיך הנבאים להוציא את עצמות מלכינו ואת עצמות אבותינו
25   ממקומם(ן) : והנך משלכות לחרב ביום ולקרח בלילה וימתו בתחלאים
26   (בנגעים) רעים ברעב בחרב ובדבר : ותתן את הבית אשר נקרא שמך עליו

Dan 9.18	כי לא על צדקתינו אנחנו מפילים תחנונינו לפניך	19
Ps 78.49	ישלח בם חרון אפו	20
Jer 26.5	לשמע על דברי עבדי הנבאים אשר אנכי שלח אליכם	
Jer 27.12	הביאו את צואריכם בעל מלך בבל ועבדו אתו	21
Jer 27.9	אל תשמעו אל נביאיכם ... אשר הם אמרים אליכם לאמר לא תעבדו את מלך בבל	22
Jer 7.34	והשבתי מערי יהודה ומחצות ירושלם קול ששון וקול שמחה קול חתן וקול כלה כי לחרבה תהיה הארץ	23
Jer 48.9	לשמה תהיינה מאין יושב בהן	
Jer 8.1	ויוציאו את עצמות מלכי יהודה ... מקבריהם	24
Jer 36.30	ונבלתו תהיה משלכת לחרב ביום ולקרח בלילה	25
Jer 16.4	ממותי תחלאים^j ימתו ... ובחרב וברעב יכלו והיתה נבלתם למאכל לעוף השמים ולבהמת הארץ	
Jer 32.36	בחרב וברעב ובדבר^j	

---

root ראב which the translator avoided by reading רעב through an interchange of both <u>daleth/resh</u> (graphical) and <u>aleph/'ayin</u> (phonetic).

^{i} ἔξωθεν ('outside') of the LXX is a mistranslation of חֻצוֹת which recurs nine times in the LXX of Jer. See above, "INTRODUCTION" section (3).

^{j} Cf. the LXX of this verse.

of the wickedness of the house of Israel and the house of Judah.

.27 Yet you have treated us, O Lord our God, with all your goodness and
.28 great mercy, as you promised through your servant Moses on the day
when you commanded him to write your Law in the presence of the children
.29 of Israel, saying: "If you do not obey me, this very great multitude
will be reduced to a small number among the nations where I shall
.30 banish them. For I know that they will not obey me - because they
are a stiffnecked people - but in the land of their captivity they will
.31 repent, acknowledging that I am the Lord their God. I shall give
.32 them a heart and ears that hear, and they will praise me in the land
.33 of their captivity and will remember my name, and they will turn from
their stubbornness and wickedness because they will remember what
.34 became of their ancestors who sinned against the Lord. I shall then
bring them back to the land which I swore to give to their forefathers,
Abraham, Isaac and Jacob, and they will take possession of it; I shall
.35 increase their number and they will not be diminished. And I shall
make an everlasting covenant with them that I shall be their God and

---

ἔρημον^k ὡς ἡ ἡμέρα αὕτη διὰ πονηρίαν οἴκου Ισραηλ καὶ οἴκου Ιουδα.

.27 Καὶ ἐποίησας εἰς ἡμᾶς, κύριε ὁ θεὸς ἡμῶν, κατὰ πᾶσαν ἐπι-
.28 είκειάν σου καὶ κατὰ πάντα οἰκτιρμόν σου τὸν μέγαν, καθὰ
ἐλάλησας ἐν χειρὶ παιδός σου Μωυσῆ ἐν ἡμέρᾳ ἐντειλαμένου σου
.29 αὐτῷ γράψαι τὸν νόμον σου ἐναντίον υἱῶν Ισραηλ λέγων Ἐὰν μὴ
ἀκούσητε τῆς φωνῆς μου, εἶ μὴν ἡ βόμβησις ἡ μεγάλη ἡ πολλὴ
αὕτη ἀποστρέψει εἰς μικρὰν ἐν τοῖς ἔθνεσιν, οὗ διασπερῶ αὐτοὺς
.30 ἐκεῖ· ὅτι ἔγνων ὅτι οὐ μὴ ἀκούσωσί μου, ὅτι λαὸς σκληροτράχη-
λός ἐστι. καὶ ἐπιστρέψουσιν ἐπὶ καρδίαν αὐτῶν ἐν γῇ ἀποικισμοῦ
.31 αὐτῶν καὶ γνώσονται ὅτι ἐγὼ κύριος ὁ θεὸς αὐτῶν. καὶ δώσω αὐ-
.32 τοῖς καρδίαν καὶ ὦτα ἀκούοντα, καὶ αἰνέσουσί με ἐν γῇ ἀποικισ-
.33 μοῦ αὐτῶν καὶ μνησθήσονται τοῦ ὀνόματός μου καὶ ἀποστρέψουσιν
ἀπὸ νώτου αὐτῶν τοῦ σκληροῦ καὶ ἀπὸ πονηρῶν πραγμάτων αὐτῶν,
ὅτι μνησθήσονται τῆς ὁδοῦ πατέρων αὐτῶν τῶν ἁμαρτόντων ἔναντι
.34 κυρίου. καὶ ἀποστρέψω αὐτοὺς εἰς τὴν γῆν, ἣν ὤμοσα τοῖς
πατράσιν αὐτῶν τῷ Αβρααμ καὶ τῷ Ισαακ καὶ τῷ Ιακωβ, καὶ
κυριεύσουσιν αὐτῆς· καὶ πληθυνῶ αὐτούς, καὶ οὐ μὴ σμικρυνθῶσι·
.35 καὶ στήσω αὐτοῖς διαθήκην αἰώνιον τοῦ εἶναί με αὐτοῖς εἰς θεὸν

27 לחרבה(לשממה)^k כיום הזה בגלל רעת בית ישראל ובית יהודה:
ותעש עמנו ה' אלהינו ככל חסדך וככל רחמיך הרבים: כאשר דברת
28 ביד עבדך משה ביום צותך אתו לכתב את תורתך לפני בני ישראל לאמר:
29 אם לא תשמעו בקולי כי ההמון הגדול הרב הזה ישוב למעט בגוים אשר
30 אדיחם שם: כי ידעתי כי לא ישמעו אלי כי עם קשה ערף הוא וישיבו אל
31 לבבם בארץ שבים: וידעו כי אני ה' אלהיהם ונתתי להם לב ואזן שמעת
32-33 (קשובה): ויודו לי בארץ שבים ויזכרו שמי: וישבו מערפם הקשה
(מקשי ערפם) ומרע מעלליהם כי יזכרו את דרך אבותם החטאים לה' (לפני
34 ה'): והשיבתים אל הארץ אשר נשבעתי לאבותם לאברהם (ו)ליצחק וליעקב
35 וירשוה והרביתים ולא ימעטו: וכרתי להם ברית עולם להיות להם

26	בגלל רעת בית ישראל ובית יהודה	Jer 11.17
	ותהיינה לחרבה לשממה כיום הזה	Jer 44.6
27	עשה עם עבדך כחסדך	Ps 119.124
28	ויכתב ... את משנה תורת משה אשר כתב לפני בני ישראל	Josh 8.32
29	והיה אם לא תשמע בקול ה' אלהיך	Deut 28.15
	נשארנו מעט מהרבה	Jer 42.2
	בכל המקמות אשר אדיחם שם	Jer 24.9
30	והשיבו אל לבבם בארץ אשר נשבו שם ... בארץ שבים	2 Chr 6.37
31	ונתתי להם לב לדעת אתי כי אני ה' ... ואנכי אהיה להם לאלהים	Jer 24.7
33	שובו נא איש מדרכו הרעה ומרע מעלליכם	Jer 25.5
34	והשבתים אל הארץ אשר נתתי לאבותם וירשוה	Jer 30.3
	ורבו שם ואל תמעטו	Jer 29.6
35	וכרתי להם ברית עולם	Jer 32.40
	כי זאת הברית אשר אכרת ... והייתי להם לאלהים והמה יהיו לי לעם	Jer 31.33

---

^{k} Based on the minority reading ἔρημον, which Ziegler and many MSS omit.

they will be my people, and I shall no more uproot my people Israel
from the land which I have given to them.

3.1 O Lord of Hosts, God of Israel, a soul in anguish and a troubled
.2 spirit cry to you. Listen, O Lord, and have mercy upon us, because we
.3 have sinned against you. You live for ever but we perish continually.
.4 O Lord of Hosts, God of Israel, listen to the prayer of the dead ones of
Israel and of the children of those who sinned against you and who did
.5 not obey the Lord their God so that the evil has clung to us. Remember
not the iniquities of our ancestors but remember your power and your name
.6 at this time. For you are the Lord our God, and we shall praise you, o
.7 Lord. You have put fear of you in our hearts that we would call upon
your name, we shall therefore praise you in our captivity, reminding
ourselves of all the wrongdoing of our ancestors who sinned against
.8 you. Behold, in our captivity where you have banished us we are at
this day an object of reproach, curse and repugnance because of all the
iniquities of our ancestors who rebelled against the Lord our God.

καὶ αὐτοὶ ἔσονταί μοι εἰς λαόν· καὶ οὐ κινήσω ἔτι τὸν λαόν μου
Ισραηλ ἀπὸ τῆς γῆς, ἧς ἔδωκα αὐτοῖς.

3.1 Κύριε παντοκράτωρ ὁ θεὸς Ισραηλ, ψυχὴ ἐν στενοῖς καὶ
.2 πνεῦμα ἀκηδιῶν κέκραγε πρὸς σέ. ἄκουσον, κύριε, καὶ ἐλέησον,
.3 ὅτι ἡμάρτομεν ἐναντίον σου· ὅτι σὺ καθήμενος τὸν αἰῶνα, καὶ
.4 ἡμεῖς ἀπολλύμενοι τὸν αἰῶνα. κύριε παντοκράτωρ ὁ θεὸς
Ισραηλ, ἄκουσον δὴ τῆς προσευχῆς τῶν τεθνηκότων Ισραηλ καὶ
υἱῶν τῶν ἁμαρτανόντων ἐναντίον σου, οἳ οὐκ ἤκουσαν τῆς φωνῆς
.5 κυρίου θεοῦ αὐτῶν, καὶ ἐκολλήθη ἡμῖν τὰ κακά. μὴ μνησθῇς
ἀδικιῶν πατέρων ἡμῶν, ἀλλὰ μνήσθητι χειρός σου καὶ ὀνόματός
.6 σου ἐν τῷ καιρῷ τούτῳ· ὅτι σὺ κύριος ὁ θεὸς ἡμῶν, καὶ αἰνέ-
.7 σομέν σε, κύριε. ὅτι διὰ τοῦτο ἔδωκας τὸν φόβον σου ἐπὶ
καρδίαν ἡμῶν τοῦ ἐπικαλεῖσθαι τὸ ὄνομά σου, καὶ αἰνέσομέν σε
ἐν τῇ ἀποικίᾳ ἡμῶν, ὅτι ἀπεστρέψαμεν ἐπὶ καρδίαν ἡμῶν πᾶσαν
.8 ἀδικίαν πατέρων ἡμῶν τῶν ἡμαρτηκότων ἐναντίον σου. ἰδοὺ
ἡμεῖς σήμερον ἐν τῇ ἀποικίᾳ ἡμῶν, οὗ διέσπειρας ἡμᾶς ἐκεῖ εἰς
ὀνειδισμὸν καὶ εἰς ἀρὰν καὶ εἰς ὄφλησιν κατὰ πάσας τὰς ἀδικίας
πατέρων ἡμῶν, οἳ ἀπέστησαν ἀπὸ κυρίου θεοῦ ἡμῶν.

3.1-8

לאלהים והמה יהיו לי לעם ולא אתוש עוד את עמי ישראל מעל האדמה אשר
נתתי להם :

3.1   ה' צבאות אלהי ישראל נפש בצרה ורוח עטופה   קראה (צעקה) אליך :

2-3   שמע ה' וחננו[1] כי חטאנו לך (לפניך) : כי אתה שכן עד ואנחנו אבדי

4   עד : ה' צבאות אלהי ישראל שמע נא אל תפלת מתי ישראל ובני החטאים

5   לך (לפניך) אשר לא שמעו בקול ה' אלהיהם ותדבק בנו הרעה : אל תזכר

6   עונות אבותינו כי זכר ידך ושמך בעת הזאת : כי אתה ה' אלהינו ונודך

7   ה' : כי על כן נתת (את) יראתך על לבבנו לקרא בשמך ונודך בשבינו כי

8   השיבנו אל לבבנו כל עון אבותינו החטאים לך (לפניך) : הנה אנחנו
      היום בשבינו אשר הדחתנו שם לחרפה ולאלה ולזועה (ולזעוה) ככל עונות
      אבותינו אשר פשעו בה' אלהינו :

___

35   ונתש את ישראל מעל האדמה הטובה הזאת אשר נתן לאבותיהם   1 Kgs 14.15

1   נפשם בהם תתעטף : ויצעקו אל ה' בצר להם   Ps 107.5-6
2   שמע ה' קולי אקרא וחנני וענני   Ps 27.7
3   שכן עד   Isa 57.15
      תאבד לעד   Ps 9.19
4   See the parallels to Bar 1.20
5   אל תזכר לנו עונת ראשנים   Ps 79.8
7   ואת יראתי אתן בלבבם   Jer 32.40
      וידעת היום והשבת אל לבבך   Deut 4.39
8   ונתתים לזועה (לזעוה : Q) לרעה לכל ממלכות הארץ לחרפה   Jer 24.9
      ולמשל לשנינה ולקללה בכל המקמות אשר אדיחם שם
      עונותיהם אשר חטאו לי ואשר פשעו בי   Jer 33.8

___

[1] The pronominal suffix has been added in the reconstruction although it
is not represented in the LXX: In the O.T. חנן usually governs an object and
its imperative and jussive forms <u>always</u> govern an object.

.9 Ἄκουε, Ισραηλ, ἐντολὰς ζωῆς, ἐνωτίσασθε γνῶναι φρόνησιν.
.10 τί ἐστιν, Ισραηλ, τί ὅτι ἐν γῇ τῶν ἐχθρῶν εἶ, ἐπαλαιώθης ἐν γῇ
.11 ἀλλοτρίᾳ, συνεμιάνθης τοῖς νεκροῖς, προσελογίσθης μετὰ τῶν
.12-3 εἰς ᾅδου; ἐγκατέλιπες τὴν πηγὴν τῆς σοφίας. τῇ ὁδῷ τοῦ
.14 θεοῦ εἰ ἐπορεύθης, κατῴκεις ἂν ἐν εἰρήνῃ τὸν αἰῶνα. μάθε ποῦ ἐστι φρόνησις; ποῦ ἐστιν ἰσχύς, ποῦ ἐστι σύνεσις τοῦ γνῶναι ἅμα, ποῦ ἐστι μακροβίωσις καὶ ζωή, ποῦ ἐστι φῶς ὀφθαλμῶν καὶ εἰρήνη.

.15 Τίς εὗρε τὸν τόπον αὐτῆς, καὶ τίς εἰσῆλθεν εἰς τοὺς θησαυ-
.16 ροὺς αὐτῆς; ποῦ εἰσιν οἱ ἄρχοντες τῶν ἐθνῶν καὶ οἱ κυριεύοντες
.17 τῶν θηρίων τῶν ἐπὶ τῆς γῆς, οἱ ἐν τοῖς ὀρνέοις τοῦ οὐρανοῦ ἐμπαίζοντες καὶ τὸ ἀργύριον θησαυρίζοντες καὶ τὸ χρυσίον, ᾧ ἐπεποίθεισαν ἄνθρωποι, καὶ οὐκ ἔστι τέλος τῆς κτήσεως αὐτῶν,
.18 οἱ τὸ ἀργύριον τεκταίνοντες καὶ μεριμνῶντες, καὶ οὐκ ἔστιν
.19 ἐξεύρεσις τῶν ἔργων αὐτῶν; ἠφανίσθησαν καὶ εἰς ᾅδου κατέβη-
.20 σαν, καὶ ἄλλοι ἀντανέστησαν ἀντ' αὐτῶν. νεώτεροι εἶδον φῶς καὶ κατῴκησαν ἐπὶ τῆς γῆς, ὁδὸν δὲ ἐπιστήμης οὐκ ἔγνωσαν
.21 οὐδὲ συνῆκαν τρίβους αὐτῆς οὐδὲ ἀντελάβοντο αὐτῆς· οἱ υἱοὶ
.22 αὐτῶν ἀπὸ τῆς ὁδοῦ αὐτῶν πόρρω ἐγενήθησαν. οὐδὲ ἠκούσθη ἐν
.23 Χανααν οὐδὲ ὤφθη ἐν Θαιμαν, οὔτε υἱοὶ Αγαρ οἱ ἐκζητοῦντες τὴν σύνεσιν ἐπὶ τῆς γῆς, οἱ ἔμποροι τῆς Μερραν καὶ Θαιμαν καὶ οἱ μυθολόγοι καὶ οἱ ἐκζητηταὶ τῆς συνέσεως, ὁδὸν δὲ σοφίας οὐκ ἔγνωσαν οὐδὲ ἐμνήσθησαν τὰς τρίβους αὐτῆς.

.24 Ὦ Ισραηλ, ὡς μέγας ὁ οἶκος τοῦ θεοῦ καὶ ἐπιμήκης ὁ τόπος
.25 τῆς κτήσεως αὐτοῦ· μέγας καὶ οὐκ ἔχει τελευτήν, ὑψηλὸς καὶ
.26 ἀμέτρητος. ἐκεῖ ἐγεννήθησαν οἱ γίγαντες οἱ ὀνομαστοὶ οἱ ἀπ'
.27 ἀρχῆς, γενόμενοι εὐμεγέθεις, ἐπιστάμενοι πόλεμον. οὐ τού-
.28 τους ἐξελέξατο ὁ θεὸς οὐδὲ ὁδὸν ἐπιστήμης ἔδωκεν αὐτοῖς· καὶ ἀπώλοντο παρὰ τὸ μὴ ἔχειν φρόνησιν, ἀπώλοντο διὰ τὴν ἀβουλίαν αὐτῶν.

.29 Τίς ἀνέβη εἰς τὸν οὐρανὸν καὶ ἔλαβεν αὐτὴν καὶ κατεβίβασεν
.30 αὐτὴν ἐκ τῶν νεφελῶν; τίς διέβη πέραν τῆς θαλάσσης καὶ εὗρεν

.9 Listen, O Israel, to the commandments that bring life; listen in
.10 order to know wisdom. Why is it, O Israel, why is it that you are in the
.11 land of your enemies, that you have grown old in a foreign country, that
you are defiled with the dead, that you are counted among those in the
.12-3 grave? Because you have forsaken the fountain of wisdom. Had you walked
.14 in the way of God, you would have lived in peace for ever. Learn where
knowledge is, where strength, where understanding, and so learn where
length of days is, where life, where the light of the eyes, and where peace.
.15 Who has found her place? And who has entered her treasure houses?
.16 Where are the rulers of the nations, and those who rule (even) the beasts
.17 of the earth; where are those who sport with the birds of heaven, and
those who accumulate silver and gold, in which men trust, and there is no
.18 limit to their possessions; where are those who carefully wrought in
.19 silver and their masterpieces are beyond imagination? They have vanished,
.20 gone down to their graves, and others have risen to take their place. A
younger generation has seen light and has dwelt upon the earth; but the
.21 way to knowledge has not been known to them. They have not understood her
paths, nor did they have a grasp of her. Their sons were far away from
.22 their path. She has not been heard of in Canaan, nor has she been seen
.23 in Teman. Neither the sons of Hagar, who seek for understanding on the
earth, the merchants of Merran and Teman, nor the story-tellers and the
seekers of understanding, knew the way to wisdom, or remembered the paths
she treads.
.24 O Israel, how great is the house of God and how vast the territory of
.25 his possession. It is great and has no end; it is high and immeasurable.
.26 In it were born the giants who were famous from antiquity, great in stature,
.27 expert in war. God's choice did not fall on these, nor did he reveal to
.28 them the way of knowledge; so they perished for lack of wisdom, they
perished in their own folly.
.29 Who has ever gone up to heaven, caught her and brought her down from
.30 the clouds? Who has ever crossed the sea, found her, and brought her back

.31 αὐτὴν καὶ οἴσει αὐτὴν χρυσίου ἐκλεκτοῦ; οὐκ ἔστιν ὁ γινώσκων
.32 τὴν ὁδὸν αὐτῆς οὐδὲ ὁ ἐνθυμούμενος τὴν τρίβον αὐτῆς· ἀλλὰ ὁ
εἰδὼς τὰ πάντα γινώσκει αὐτήν, ἐξεῦρεν αὐτὴν τῇ συνέσει αὐτοῦ·
ὁ κατασκευάσας τὴν γῆν εἰς τὸν αἰῶνα χρόνον, ἐνέπλησεν αὐτὴν
.33 κτηνῶν τετραπόδων· ὁ ἀποστέλλων τὸ φῶς, καὶ πορεύεται,
.34 ἐκάλεσεν αὐτό, καὶ ὑπήκουσεν αὐτῷ τρόμῳ· οἱ δὲ ἀστέρες
.35 ἔλαμψαν ἐν ταῖς φυλακαῖς αὐτῶν καὶ εὐφράνθησαν, ἐκάλεσεν
αὐτούς, καὶ εἶπαν Πάρεσμεν, ἔλαμψαν μετ'εὐφροσύνης τῷ ποιήσαν-
.36 τι αὐτούς. οὗτος ὁ θεὸς ἡμῶν, οὐ λογισθήσεται ἕτερος πρὸς
.37 αὐτόν. ἐξεῦρε πᾶσαν ὁδὸν ἐπιστήμης καὶ ἔδωκεν αὐτὴν Ιακωβ
.38 τῷ παιδὶ αὐτοῦ καὶ Ισραηλ τῷ ἠγαπημένῳ ὑπ'αὐτοῦ· μετὰ τοῦτο
ἐπὶ τῆς γῆς ὤφθη καὶ ἐν τοῖς ἀνθρώποις συνανεστράφη.
4.1 Αὕτη ἡ βίβλος τῶν προσταγμάτων τοῦ θεοῦ καὶ ὁ **νόμος** ὁ
ὑπάρχων εἰς τὸν αἰῶνα· πάντες οἱ κρατοῦντες αὐτὴν εἰς ζωήν, οἱ
.2 δὲ καταλείποντες αὐτὴν ἀποθανοῦνται. ἐπιστρέφου, Ιακωβ, καὶ
ἐπιλαβοῦ αὐτῆς, διόδευσον πρὸς τὴν λάμψιν κατέναντι τοῦ φωτὸς
.3 αὐτῆς. μὴ δῷς ἑτέρῳ τὴν δόξαν σου καὶ τὰ συμφέροντά σοι ἔθ-
.4 νει ἀλλοτρίῳ. μακάριοί ἐσμεν, Ισραηλ, ὅτι τὰ ἀρεστὰ τῷ θεῷ
ἡμῖν γνωστά ἐστιν.
.5-6 Θαρσεῖτε, λαός μου, μνημόσυνον Ισραηλ. ἐπράθητε τοῖς
ἔθνεσιν οὐκ εἰς ἀπώλειαν, διὰ δὲ τὸ παροργίσαι ὑμᾶς τὸν θεὸν
.7 παρεδόθητε τοῖς ὑπεναντίοις· παρωξύνατε γὰρ τὸν ποιήσαντα
.8 ὑμᾶς θύσαντες δαιμονίοις καὶ οὐ θεῷ. ἐπελάθεσθε δὲ τὸν τρο-
φεύσαντα ὑμᾶς θεὸν αἰώνιον, ἐλυπήσατε δὲ καὶ τὴν ἐκθρέψασαν
.9 ὑμᾶς Ιερουσαλημ· εἶδε γὰρ τὴν ἐπελθοῦσαν ὑμῖν ὀργὴν παρὰ
τοῦ θεοῦ καὶ εἶπεν Ἀκούσατε, αἱ πάροικοι Σιων, ἐπήγαγέ μοι ὁ
.10 θεὸς πένθος μέγα· εἶδον γὰρ τὴν αἰχμαλωσίαν τῶν υἱῶν μου
.11 καὶ θυγατέρων, ἣν ἐπήγαγεν αὐτοῖς ὁ αἰώνιος· ἔθρεψα γὰρ αὐτοὺς μετ'εὐφροσύνης, ἐξαπέστειλα δὲ μετὰ κλαυθμοῦ καὶ πένθους.
.12 μηδεὶς ἐπιχαιρέτω μοι τῇ χήρᾳ καὶ καταλειφθείσῃ ὑπὸ πολλῶν·
ἠρημώθην διὰ τὰς ἁμαρτίας τῶν τέκνων μου, διότι ἐξέκλιναν ἐκ
.13 νόμου θεοῦ καὶ δικαιώματα αὐτοῦ οὐκ ἔγνωσαν οὐδὲ ἐπορεύθησαν

.31	in exchange for pure gold? No one knows her way or can discover the
.32	path she treads. But he who knows all knows her, he has found her
	by his own understanding. He who established the earth for all time
.33	filled it with four-footed beasts; he sends forth the light, and it
.34	goes; he calls it back, and it obeys him in fear; the stars shine
.35	at their watches, and are glad; when he calls them, they answer:
.36	"Here we are!" They shine gladly for their creator. This is our
.37	God; no other can be considered worthy beside him. He found the
	whole way of knowledge, and gave it to Jacob his servant and to
.38	Israel, whom he loved. Afterwards she appeared upon earth and moved
	among men.
4.1	This is the book of the commandments of God, the law that en-
.2	dures for ever. All who keep her will live, but those who forsake her
	will die. Turn back, O Jacob, seize her; walk towards her shining
.3	in her radiance. Do not give your glory to another, or your advan-
.4	tages to an alien people. Happy are we, O Israel, for what is
	pleasing to God has been made known to us.
.5-6	Take courage, my people, O constant reminder of Israel. You
	were sold to the nations, though not to be destroyed; because you
.7	angered God you were handed over to your enemies. For you provoked
.8	your creator by sacrificing to demons, not to God. You had forgotten
	the everlasting God who nurtured you, and you had also grieved Jeru-
.9	salem who reared you. For when she saw how the wrath came upon you
	from God, she said: "Listen, you neighbors of Zion, God has brought
.10	great sorrow upon me; for I have seen my sons and daughters taken
.11	into captivity, which the Everlasting has brought upon them. For I
	had nurtured them joyfully, but I saw them go with tears and in sorrow.
.12	Let no one rejoice over me, a widow, forsaken by many; I was left
	desolate because of the sins of my own children, because they turned
.13	away from the Law of God and because they did not want to know his

.14 ὁδοῖς ἐντολῶν θεοῦ οὐδὲ τρίβους παιδείας ἐν δικαιοσύνῃ αὐτοῦ ἐπέβησαν. ἐλθάτωσαν αἱ πάροικοι Σιων, καὶ μνήσθητε τὴν αἰχμαλωσίαν τῶν υἱῶν μου καὶ θυγατέρων, ἥν ἐπήγαγεν αὐτοῖς ὁ
.15 αἰώνιος· ἐπήγαγε γὰρ ἐπ'αὐτοὺς ἔθνος μακρόθεν, ἔθνος ἀναιδὲς καὶ ἀλλόγλωσσον, οἳ οὐκ ᾐσχύνθησαν πρεσβύτην οὐδὲ παιδίον
.16 ἠλέησαν καὶ ἀπήγαγον τοὺς ἀγαπητοὺς τῆς χήρας καὶ ἀπὸ τῶν
.17 θυγατέρων τὴν μόνην ἠρήμωσαν. ἐγὼ δὲ τί δυνατὴ βοηθῆσαι
.18 ὑμῖν; ὁ γὰρ ἐπαγαγὼν τὰ κακὰ ἐξελεῖται ὑμᾶς ἐκ χειρὸς
.19 ἐχθρῶν ὑμῶν. βαδίζετε, τέκνα, βαδίζετε, ἐγὼ γὰρ κατελείφθην
.20 ἔρημος· ἐξεδυσάμην τὴν στολὴν τῆς εἰρήνης, ἐνεδυσάμην δὲ σάκκον τῆς δεήσεώς μου, κεκράξομαι πρὸς τὸν αἰώνιον ἐν ταῖς ἡμέραις μου.
.21 Θαρσεῖτε, τέκνα, βοήσατε πρὸς τὸν θεόν, καὶ ἐξελεῖται
.22 ὑμᾶς ἐκ δυναστείας, ἐκ χειρὸς ἐχθρῶν. ἐγὼ γὰρ ἤλπισα ἐπὶ τῷ αἰωνίῳ τὴν σωτηρίαν ὑμῶν, καὶ ἦλθέ μοι χαρὰ παρὰ τοῦ ἁγίου ἐπὶ τῇ ἐλεημοσύνῃ, ἣ ἥξει ὑμῖν ἐν τάχει παρὰ τοῦ αἰωνίου
.23 σωτῆρος ὑμῶν. ἐξέπεμψα γὰρ ὑμᾶς μετὰ πένθους καὶ κλαυθμοῦ, ἀποδώσει δέ μοι ὁ θεὸς ὑμᾶς μετὰ χαρμοσύνης καὶ εὐφροσύνης εἰς
.24 τὸν αἰῶνα. ὥσπερ γὰρ νῦν ἑοράκασιν αἱ πάροικοι Σιων τὴν ὑμετέραν αἰχμαλωσίαν, οὕτως ὄψονται ἐν τάχει τὴν παρὰ τοῦ θεοῦ ὑμῶν σωτηρίαν, ἣ ἐπελεύσεται ὑμῖν μετὰ δόξης μεγάλης καὶ λαμ-
.25 πρότητος τοῦ αἰωνίου. τέκνα, μακροθυμήσατε τὴν παρὰ τοῦ θεοῦ ἐπελθοῦσαν ὑμῖν ὀργήν· κατεδίωξέ σε ὁ ἐχθρός, καὶ ὄψει αὐτοῦ τὴν ἀπώλειαν ἐν τάχει καὶ ἐπὶ τραχήλους αὐτῶν ἐπιβήσῃ.
.26 οἱ τρυφεροί μου ἐπορεύθησαν ὁδοὺς τραχείας, ἤρθησαν ὡς ποίμνιον ἡρπασμένον ὑπὸ ἐχθρῶν.
.27 Θαρσήσατε, τέκνα, καὶ βοήσατε πρὸς τὸν θεόν, ἔσται γὰρ
.28 ὑμῶν ὑπὸ τοῦ ἐπάγοντος μνεία. ὥσπερ γὰρ ἐγένετο ἡ διάνοια ὑμῶν εἰς τὸ πλανηθῆναι ἀπὸ τοῦ θεοῦ, δεκαπλασιάσατε ἐπιστρα-
.29 φέντες ζητῆσαι αὐτόν. ὁ γὰρ ἐπαγαγὼν ὑμῖν τὰ κακὰ ἐπάξει ὑμῖν τὴν αἰώνιον εὐφροσύνην μετὰ τῆς σωτηρίας ὑμῶν.

	statutes and did not walk in the ways of God's commandments, nor

.14   tread the paths of discipline as required by his justice. Let them
come, the neighbors of Zion; remember the captivity of my sons and
.15   daughters, which the Everlasting has brought upon them. For he brought
upon them a nation from far away, a ruthless nation speaking a strange
language, who had neither respect for old men nor pity for children.
.16   They led away the widow's beloved sons, and bereaved the lonely woman
.17-8 of her daughters. But I, how can I help you? For he who brought
the disasters upon you, he is the one to deliver you from the hands
.19   of your enemies. Go, my children, go your way; for I have been left
.20   desolate. I have taken off the robe of peace and put on the sack-
cloth of supplication; I will cry to the Everlasting all my life.

.21   Take courage, my children, cry to God; he will deliver you from
.22   tyranny, from the hands of your enemies. For I have put my hope in
the Everlasting to save you, and joy has come to me from the Holy One,
because of the mercy which soon will reach you from your everlasting
.23   savior. For I saw you go away in sorrow and with tears, but God will
.24   give you back to me in joy and gladness forever. For as the neighbors
of Zion have now seen your captivity, so will they soon see your sal-
vation by God, which will come to you with great glory and with the
.25   splendor of the Everlasting. My children, endure with patience the
wrath that God has brought upon you. Your enemy has persecuted you,
but you will soon witness his destruction and tread upon his neck.
.26   My tender ones have trodden on rough roads; they were carried away like
a flock overpowered by enemies.

.27   Take courage, my children, and cry to God, for you will be
.28   remembered by him who brought disaster upon you. For just as you
first resolved to go astray from God, return with tenfold zeal to seek
.29   him. For he who brought those disasters upon you will bring you
everlasting joy when he rescues you.

.30-31 Θάρσει, Ιερουσαλημ, παρακαλέσει σε ὁ ὀνομάσας σε. δεί-
.32 λαιοι οἱ σὲ κακώσαντες καὶ ἐπιχάραντες τῇ σῇ πτώσει, δεί-
λαιαι αἱ πόλεις αἷς ἐδούλευσαν τὰ τέκνα σου, δειλαία ἡ δεξα-
.33 μένη τοὺς υἱούς σου. ὥσπερ γὰρ ἐχάρη ἐπὶ τῇ σῇ πτώσει καὶ
εὐφράνθη ἐπὶ τῷ πτώματί σου, οὕτως λυπηθήσεται ἐπὶ τῇ ἑαυτῆς
.34 ἐρημίᾳ. καὶ περιελῶ αὐτῆς τὸ ἀγαλλίαμα τῆς πολυοχλίας, καὶ
.35 τὸ ἀγαυρίαμα αὐτῆς ἔσται εἰς πένθος. πῦρ γὰρ ἐπελεύσεται
αὐτῇ παρὰ τοῦ αἰωνίου εἰς ἡμέρας μακράς, καὶ κατοικηθήσεται
ὑπὸ δαιμονίων τὸν πλείονα χρόνον.
.36 Περίβλεψαι πρὸς ἀνατολάς, Ιερουσαλημ, καὶ ἴδε τὴν εὐφρο-
.37 σύνην τὴν παρὰ τοῦ θεοῦ σοι ἐρχομένην. ἰδοὺ ἔρχονται οἱ
υἱοί σου, οὓς ἐξαπέστειλας, ἔρχονται συνηγμένοι ἀπὸ ἀνατολῶν
ἕως δυσμῶν τῷ ῥήματι τοῦ ἁγίου χαίροντες τῇ τοῦ θεοῦ δόξῃ.
5.1 Ἔκδυσαι, Ιερουσαλημ, τὴν στολὴν τοῦ πένθους καὶ τῆς
κακώσεώς σου καὶ ἔνδυσαι τὴν εὐπρέπειαν τῆς παρὰ τοῦ θεοῦ
.2 δόξης εἰς τὸν αἰῶνα. περιβαλοῦ τὴν διπλοΐδα τῆς παρὰ τοῦ
θεοῦ δικαιοσύνης, ἐπίθου τὴν μίτραν ἐπὶ τὴν κεφαλήν σου τῆς
.3 δόξης τοῦ αἰωνίου. ὁ γὰρ θεὸς δείξει τῇ ὑπ'οὐρανὸν πάσῃ
.4 τὴν σὴν λαμπρότητα. κληθήσεται γάρ σου τὸ ὄνομα παρὰ τοῦ
θεοῦ εἰς τὸν αἰῶνα Εἰρήνη δικαιοσύνης καὶ δόξα θεοσεβείας.
.5 Ἀνάστηθι, Ιερουσαλημ, καὶ στῆθι ἐπὶ τοῦ ὑψηλοῦ καὶ περίβλεψαι πρὸς ἀνατολὰς καὶ ἴδε σου συνηγμένα τὰ τέκνα ἀπὸ ἡλίου
δυσμῶν ἕως ἀνατολῶν τῷ ῥήματι τοῦ ἁγίου χαίροντας τῇ τοῦ θεοῦ
.6 μνείᾳ. ἐξῆλθον γὰρ παρὰ σοῦ πεζοὶ ἀγόμενοι ὑπὸ ἐχθρῶν, εἰσ-
άγει δὲ αὐτοὺς ὁ θεὸς πρὸς σὲ αἰρομένους μετὰ δόξης ὡς θρόνον
.7 βασιλείας. συνέταξε γὰρ ὁ θεὸς ταπεινοῦσθαι πᾶν ὄρος ὑψη-
λὸν καὶ θῖνας ἀενάους καὶ φάραγγας πληροῦσθαι εἰς ὁμαλισμὸν
.8 τῆς γῆς, ἵνα βαδίσῃ Ισραηλ ἀσφαλῶς τῇ τοῦ θεοῦ δόξῃ· ἐσκία-
σαν δὲ καὶ οἱ δρυμοὶ καὶ πᾶν ξύλον εὐωδίας τῷ Ισραηλ προστάγ-
.9 ματι τοῦ θεοῦ· ἡγήσεται γὰρ ὁ θεὸς Ισραηλ μετ'εὐφροσύνης
τῷ φωτὶ τῆς δόξης αὐτοῦ σὺν ἐλεημοσύνῃ καὶ δικαιοσύνῃ τῇ παρ'
αὐτοῦ.

.30 Take courage, O Jerusalem, for he who named you will comfort you.
.31 Wretched will be those who afflicted you and rejoiced at your fall.
.32 Wretched will be the cities which your children served as slaves;
.33 wretched will be the city which received your sons. For just as she rejoiced at your fall and was glad to see your ruin, so will she be
.34 grieved at her own desolation. And I will deprive her of her pride in her great population, and her boasting will be turned into grief.
.35 For fire will come upon her from the Everlasting for many days, and for a long time she will be inhabited by demons.
.36 Look toward the east, O Jerusalem, and see the joy that is
.37 coming to you from God. Behold, your sons are coming, whom you saw going away; they are coming, gathered from east and west, at the command of the Holy One, rejoicing in the glory of God.

5.1 Take off your garment of sorrow and affliction, O Jerusalem, and
.2 put on for ever the beauty of the glory of God. Put on the cloak of justice of God; put the diadem of the glory of the Everlasting on your
.3-4 head. For God will show your splendor everywhere under heaven. For your name will forever be called by God "Righteous peace and Godly glory".
.5 Arise, O Jerusalem, stand on the heights and look toward the east: see your children gathered from west and east, at the command of the
.6 Holy One, rejoicing that God has remembered them. For they went forth from you on foot, led away by enemies; but God will bring them
.7 back to you, carried in glory, as (on) royal thrones. For God has ordered that every high mountain and the everlasting hills be made low and that the valleys be filled to make the ground level, so that
.8 Israel may walk safely in the glory of God. The woods and every
.9 fragrant tree will provide shade for Israel at God's command. For God will lead Israel in joy by the light of his glory, with his mercy and justice beside him.

APPENDIX

Greek-Hebrew and Hebrew-Greek Concordances to Bar 1.1-3.8

The Greek-Hebrew and Hebrew-Greek concordances may be regarded as a modest supplement to the existing concordances to the LXX since these do not list the Hebrew equivalents of words in Baruch. The concordances refer to all Greek words contained in Bar 1.1-3.8 except for personal names.

Both concordances are based upon our reconstruction of Bar and consequently all equivalents listed below are tentative. As in the reconstruction itself, problematic reconstructions are underlined and at times two options are provided.

The Greek-Hebrew concordance reflects our reconstruction which is mainly based on Ziegler's text. As a result, most of the variants contained in Ziegler's apparatus are excluded from the concordance. A few major variants to Greek words reflected in our reconstruction are, however, included in the concordance; such references are written in brackets, e.g. (1.9). For details one is referred to Ziegler's apparatus.

All relevant information is provided in the Greek-Hebrew concordance, to which the Hebrew-Greek concordance serves as a reverse index.

The Hebrew concordance is arranged according to the alphabet; however, derived forms of the verb are listed with their ground-forms, e.g., הטה occurs together with נטה.

ἄβατος   שמה   2.4,23
ἅγιος   קדֹש   2.16
ἀγοράζω   קנה   1.10
ἄγω   הביא   1.9
ᾅδης   שאול   2.17
ἀδικέω   רשע   2.12
ἀδικία   עון   3.5,7,8
αἰνέω   הודה   2.32   3.6,7
αἰσχύνη   בשת   1.15   2.6
αἰών   עַד   3.3,3
αἰώνιος   עולם   2.35
ἀκηδιῶν   עָטוּף   3.1
ἀκούω   שמע   1.18,19,21   2.5,10,16,22,24,29,30   3.2,4,4
         שמע/קשב   2.31
ἀλλά   כי   2.18   3.5
ἁμαρτάνω   abs.   חטא   2.12
         + dat.   חטא ל-   1.13   2.5
         ἔναντι/ἐναντίον   חטא ל-   1.17   2.33   3.2,4,7
ἁμαρτία (περὶ ἁμαρτίας)   חטאת   1.10
ἀναγιγνώσκω   קרא   1.3,14
ἀναφέρω   העלה   1.10
ἄνθρωπος   איש   1.15   2.1,3,3
ἀνοίγνυμι   פקח   2.17
ἀπειθέω   + dat.   מרד ב-   1.18
                  המרה   1.19
ἀπό   -ב   3.8
      מאין   2.23
      מן   1.9,13   2.8,13,17,33,33
      (ל)מן   1.4,19
      מעל   2.35
(ἀπο)θνῄσκω   מות   2.17,25   3.4
ἀποικία   שבי   3.7,8
ἀποικίζω   הגלה   1.9
           שבה   2.14
ἀποικισμός   שבי   2.30,32
ἀπόλλυμαι   אבד   3.3
ἀποστέλλω   שלח   1.7,10,14,21
ἀποστολή   דְבָר   2.25
ἀποστρέφω   שוב   1.13   2.8,13,29,33
           השיב   1.8   2.34   3.7
ἀρά   אלה   1.20   3.8

ἀργύριον   כסף   1.6,10,10
ἀργυροῦς   כסף   1.8
ἄρχων   שר   1.9,16   2.1
ἀσεβέω   עוה   2.12
ἀσθενέω   כשל   2.18
αὐτός   הוא, etc. passim
ἀφίστημι ἀπό   פשע ב-   3.8
βαδίζω   הלך   2.18
βασιλεία   ממלכה   2.4
βασιλεύς   מלך   1.3,4,8,9,11,12,16   2.1,19,21,22,24,24
βιβλίον   ספר   1.1,3,14
βίβλος   ספר   1.3
βόμβησις   המון   2.29
βραχίων   זרע   2.11
γάλα   חלב   1.20
γένος   עם   2.15
γῆ   אדמה   2.35
     ארץ   1.8,9,11,19,20,20   2.11.15,21,23,30,32,34
γίγνομαι   היה   2.5
γιγνώσκω   ידע   2.15,30,31
γράφω   כתב   1.1   2.2,28
γρηγορέω   שקד   2.9
δέ   -ו   1.15   2.6
δέησις   תחנונים   2.14
δέκατος   עשרה   1.8
δέομαι   חִלָּה   2.8
δεσμώτης   מסגר   1.9
δή   נא   3.4
διά   בגלל   2.26
διὰ τοῦτο   על כן   3.7
διαθήκη   ברית   2.35
διανόημα   מחשבה/מועצה   (2.8)
διάνοια   שררות   1.22
διασπείρω   הדיח   2.4,13,29   3.8
δίδωμι   נתן   1.12,18,20   2.4,10,14,17,18,21,31,35   3.7
δικάζω   שפט   2.1
δίκαιος   צדיק   2.9
δικαιοσύνη   צדקה   1.15   2.6,18
δικαίωμα   צדק   2.13,17,19
δικαστής   שֹׁפֵט   2.1
δόξα   כבוד   2.17,18
δουλεύω   עבד   1.12
δύναμαι   השיג   1.6

δύναμις כח 2.11
δυνατός גבר 1.4,9
ἐάν אם 2.22,29
ἑβδόμη שבעה 1.2
ἔθνος גוי 2.13,29
εἰ μήν כי 2.29
εἰμι הוא 2.30; היה 1.11,19 2.23,35,35
εἶπον אמר 1.10 2.21
εἰς ∅ 1.7,9
    ב- 1.20 2.20
    בעד 1.11
    אל /-ל 1.8,11 2.4,4,16,23,29,34,35,35 3.8,8,8
    עם 2.27
εἰσάγω הביא (1.9)
εἰσακούω שמע 2.14 (2.16,30)
ἐκ מן 1.8,19,20 2.11,16,23,25
ἕκαστος איש 1.6,22 2.8
ἐκεῖ שׁם 2.4,13,29 3.8
ἐκλείπω כליון 2.18
ἔκλειψιν ποιέω השבית 2.23
ἐκρίπτομαι השליך 2.25
ἐκφέρομαι הוציא 1.8 2.24
ἐλεέω חנן 3.2
ἔλεος תחנונים 2.19
ἐμπίπρημι שרף 1.2
ἐν ב- 1.1,2,2,2,2,3,3,4,4,4,4,7,8,14,20,22 2.2,4,11,11,11,11,11,
        13,17,20,24,25,25,25,25,28,28,29,32 3.1,5,7,8
ἐν ὠσί באזני 1.3,3,4,4,4
ἔναντι לפני (1.5)
    -לפני/ל 2.33
ἐναντίον בעיני 1.12
    לפני 1.5 2.28
    -לפני/ל 1.17 3.2,4,7
ἕνεκεν למען 2.14
ἐνίημι שלח 2.20
ἐννοέω הביט/שים לב 2.16
ἐνοικέω ישב 2.23
ἐντέλλομαι צוה 2.9,28
ἐνώπιον לפני (2.28)
ἑορτή חג 1.14
ἐξαγορεύω התודה 1.14
ἐξάγω הוציא 1.19,20 2.11

ἐξαιρέω	הציל	2.14	
ἔξωθεν	חֻצות	2.23	
ἐπάγω	הביא	2.9	
ἐπάνω	למעלה	2.5	
ἐπί	+ gen.	על	1.4
	+ dat.	על	2.9,26
	+ acc.	∅	2.18
		אל	2.30 <u>3.7</u>
		ב־	(2.20)
		כ־	2.13
		על	1.10 2.1,1,1,1,1,7,7,9,9,15,15,19,21 3.7,8
ἐπιείκεια	חסד	2.27	
ἐπικαλέω	קרא	2.15,26 3.7	
ἐπιστρέφω	השיב	2.30,(33)	
ἐργάζομαι	עבד	1.22 2.21,22,24	
ἔργον	מעשה	2.9	
ἔρημος	חרבה/שממה	(2.26)	
ἔρχομαι	בא	1.3 2.7	
ἐρῶ	אמר	1.15	
ἕτερος	אחר	1.22	
ἔτι	עוד	2.35	
ἔτος	שנה	1.2	
εὑρίσκω	מצא	1.7,12	
εὐφροσύνη	ששון	2.23	
εὔχομαι	התפלל	1.5	
ἕως	עד	1.4,13,19	
ἦ μήν	כי	(2.29)	
ἡμέρα	יום	1.11,11,12,13,14,14,15,19,19,20,20 2.6,11,25,26,28	
ζῶ	חי	1.12	
ζωή	חים	1.11,11	
θεός	אלהים	1.10,13,13,15,18,19,22,22 2.5,6,11,13,15,19,27,31,35 3.1,4,4,6,8	
θυγάτηρ	בת	2.3	
θυμός	אף	1.13 2.13,20	
θυσιαστήριον	מזבח	1.10	
ἰδού	הנה	1.10 2.25 3.8	
ἱερεύς	כהן	1.7,7,16	
ἵνα	למען	1.11 2.15	
ἵστημι	הקים	2.1,24	
	כרת	2.35	
ἰσχύς	עז	1.12	
καθά	כאשר	<u>1.6</u> 2.2,28	
καθάπερ	כאשר	2.20	
κάθημαι	שכן	3.3	

καθίζω   ישב   2.21
καθοράω   השקיף   2.16
καί   -ו   passim
καιρός   מועד   1.14
         עת   1.2   3.5
κακά   רעה   1.20   2.7,9   3.4
κακός   רע   1.22
καρδία   לב   1.22   2.8,30,31   3.7,7
κατά   -כ   1.21   2.2,27,27   3.8
κατὰ πρόσωπον   לפני   1.18   2.10,14,19
κατ᾽ὀφθαλμούς   בעיני   1.22
καταβάλλω   הפיל   2.19
καταλείπομαι   נשאר   2.13
κατάρα   אלה   (3.8)
κατοικέω   ישב   1.4,15
καῦμα   חֹרב   2.25
κινέω   נחש   2.35
κλαίω   בכה   1.5
κλίνω   הטה   2.16,21
κολλάομαι   דבק   1.20   3.4
κράζω   קרא/צעק   3.1
κραταιός   חזק   2.11
κύκλῳ   סביב   2.4,4
κύπτων   <u>כפוף</u>   2.18
κυριεύω   ירש   2.34
κύριος   'ה   1.5,8,10,12,13,13,13,14,15,17,18,18,19,19,20,21,22
         2.1,4,5,6,7,8,9,9,9,10,11,13,14,15,16,16,17,17,18,
         19,27,31,33   3.1,2,4,4,6,6,8
λαλέω   דָּבַר   2.1,7,20,24,28
λαμβάνω   לכד   1.2
         לקח   1.8   2.17
λαός   גוי   2.4
         עם   1.3,4,7,9   2.11,30,35,35
λέγων   לאמר   2.20,28
λίβανος   לבונה   1.10
λιμός   רעב   2.25
λόγος   דָּבָר   1.1,3,21   2.1,24
λυπέομαι   רגז   2.18
μαναα   מנחה   1.10
μέγας   גדול   1.4   2.11,29
         רב   2.27
μέγεθος   (<u>רגל</u>)<u>גדל</u>   2.18
μέλι   דבש   1.20

μετά + gen.   עִם   1.7
      + acc. אחרי 1.9
μήν   חדש   1.2
μικρός מעט 2.29 ; קטן 1.4
μιμνήσκομαι זכר 2.32,33 3.5,5
ναός   היכל 1.8
νηστεύω צום 1.5
νόημα   מחשבה/מועצה 2.8
νόμος   תורה 2.2,28
νύμφη   כלה   2.23
νυμφίος חתן 2.23
νῦν   עתה   2.11
νύξ   לילה 2.25
νῶτον   ערף   2.33
ὁδός   דרך   2.33
οἶκος   בית   1.8,14 2.26,26,26
       מעון 2.16
οἰκτιρμός רחמים 2.27
οἴχομαι הלך 1.22
ὀλίγος   מעט 2.13
ὁλοκαύτωμα עולה 1.10
ὄμνυμι נשבע 2.34
ὀνειδισμός חרפה 2.4 3.8
ὄνομα   שֵׁם 2.11,15,26,32 3.5,7
ὁράω   ראה   2.17
ὀργή   חמה   1.13 2.20
ὅς, etc. אשר passim
ὀστοῦν   עצם 2.24,24
ὅτι   כי   1.13 2.5,9,13,17,19,20,30,30,31,33
               3.2,3,6,7,7
οὗ ... ἐκεῖ / ἐπ'αὐτῷ שם/עליו .. אשר 2.4,13,26,29 3.8
οὐκ   לא   passim
οὐρανός שמים 1.11
οὖς   אזן   1.3,3,4,4,4 2.16,31
οὗτος   זה, etc. passim
οὕτως   כה   2.21
ὀφθαλμός עין   1.12,22 2.17,18
ὄφλησις לזועה/לזעוה 3.8
παγετός קרח   2.25
παῖς   עֶבֶד 1.20 2.20,24,28
(κύριος) παντοκράτωρ צבאות (ה') 3.1,4
πᾶς   כל   passim
πατήρ   אב   1.16,19,20 2.6,19,21,24,33,34 3.5,7,8

πεινῶν   דאבון   2.18
πέμπτος   חמישי   1.2
περί + gen.   בעד   1.11,11,13
περὶ ἁμαρτίας → ἁμαρτία
πληθύνω   הרבה   2.34
πνεῦμα   רוח   2.17 3.1
ποιέω   עשה   1.8,10,22 2.2,2,11,27
πόλις   עיר   2.23
πολύς   רב   1.12 2.29
πονηρία   רעה   2.26
πονηρός   רַע   1.22 2.8,25
          רֹעַ   2.33
πόνοι   תחלאים/נגעים   2.25
πορεύομαι   הלך   1.18 2.10
ποταμός   נהר   1.4
πράγματα   מעללים   2.33
πρεσβύτερος   זקן   1.4
πρός + acc.   אל   1.3,7,7,7,10,13,14,21 3.1
             עם   1.19
πρὸς τὸ μή   לבלתי   1.19 2.5
προσευχή   תפלה   2.14 3.4
προσεύχομαι   התפלל   1.11,13
προσκολλάομαι   דבק   (3.4)
πρόσταγμα   תורה   1.18 2.10
πρόσωπον (→ κατὰ πρ.)   פנים   2.8
πρόσωπα   פנים   1.15 2.6
προφήτης   נביא   1.16,21 2.20,24
πῦρ   אש   1.2
ῥέω   זוב   1.20
ῥομφαία   חֶרֶב   2.25
σάρκες   בשר   2.3,3
σημεῖον   אה   2.11
σήμερον   היום   3.8
σκεῦος   כלי   1,8,8
σκιά   צל   1,12,12
σκληρός   קשה/קשי   2.33
σκληροτράχηλος   קשה ערף   2.30
σμικρύνομαι   מעט   2.34
σπλάγχνα   קרב   2.17
στενά   צרה   3.1
συνάγω   קבץ   1.6
συντάσσω   צוה   1.20
σχεδιάζω   סור   1.19

τέρας　　מופת　　2.11
τίθημι　　נתן　　2.26
τόπος　　מקום　　2.24
υἱός　　בן　　1.1,1,1,1,1,3,4,7,7,8,11,12　2.3,28　3.4
ὑπακούω　　שמע　　(1.19) (2.5)
ὑπό　　-ב　　1.12,12
ὑποκάτω　　למטה　　2.5
　　　　　+ gen.　תחת　　2.2
ὑποχείριος　　לזועה/לזעוה　　2.4
ὑψηλός　　נטוי　　2.11
φάγω　　אכל　　2.3
φόβος　　יראה　　3.7
φωνή　　קול　　1.18,19,21　2.5,10,22,23,23,23,23,24,29　3.4
φωτίζω　　האיר　　1.12
χάρις　　חן　　1.12　2.14
χαρμονή　　שמחה　　(2.23)
χαρμοσύνη　　שמחה　　2.23
χείρ　　יד　　1.6　2.11,20,24,28　3.5
ψυχή　　לב　　2.18
　　　　　נפש　　2.18　3.1
ὦμος　　צואר　　2.21
ὡς　　-כ　　1.11,15,20　2.6,11,26

אב	πατήρ
אבד	ἀπόλλυμαι
אדמה	γῆ
האיר	φωτίζω
אזן	οὖς
אחר	ἕτερος
אחרי	μετά
מאין → אין	
איש	ἄνθρωπος, ἕκαστος
אכל	φάγω
אל/ל-	εἰς, ἔναντι, ἐναντίον, ἐπί, περί, πρός
אלה	ἀρά
אלהים	θεός
אם	ἐάν
אמר	εἶπον, ἐρῶ
לאמר	λέγων
אף	θυμός
ארץ	γῆ
אש	πῦρ
אשר	ὅς, etc.
אשר .. שם/עליו	οὗ ... ἐκεῖ / ἐπ'αὐτῷ
אֹת	σημεῖον
ב-	ἐν, εἰς, ὑπό
בא	ἔρχομαι
הביא	ἄγω, εἰσάγω, ἐπάγω
באזני	ἐν ὡσί
בגלל	διά
בית	οἶκος
בכה	κλαίω
לבלתי → בלתי	
בן	υἱός
בעד	εἰς, περί
בעיני	ἐναντίον, κατ'ὀφθαλμούς
ברית	διαθήκη
בשר	σάρκες
בשה	αἰσχύνη
בת	θυγάτηρ
גבר	δυνατός
גדול	μέγας
גדל (רגל)	μέγεθος
גוי	ἔθνος, λαός

הגלה ἀποικίζω 47
דאבון πεινῶν
דבק (προσ)κολλάομαι
דָּבַר λαλέω
דָּבָר λόγος
דְּבֵר ἀποστολή
דבש μέλι
דרך ὁδός
ה' κύριος
היה γίγνομαι, εἰμί
היום σήμερον
היכל ναός
הלך βαδίζω, οἴχομαι, πορεύομαι
המון βόμβησις
הנה ἰδού
-ו δέ, καί
הז, etc. οὗτος, etc.
זוב ῥέω
זועה → לזועה
זכר μιμνήσκομαι
זקן πρεσβύτερος
זרע βραχίων
חג ἑορτή
חדש μήν
חזק κραταιός
חטא ἁμαρτάνω
חטאת περὶ ἁμαρτίας
חי ζῶ
חים ζωή
חלב γάλα
חלה δέομαι
חמה ὀργή
חמישי πέμπτος
חן χάρις
חנן ἐλεέω
חסד ἐπιείκεια
חצות ἔξωθεν
חרב καῦμα
חֶרֶב ῥομφαία
חרבה ἔρημος
חרפה ὀνειδισμός
חתן νυμφίος
יד χείρ
הודה αἰνέω

התודה	ἐξαγορεύω
ידע	γιγνώσκω
יום	ἡμέρα ;→ היום
הוציא	ἐκφέρομαι, ἐξάγω
יראה	φόβος
ירש	κυριεύω
ישב	ἐνοικέω, καθίζω, κατοικέω
-כ	ἐπί, κατά, ὡς
כאשר	καθά, καθάπερ
כבוד	δόξα
כה	οὕτως
כהן	ἱερεύς
כח	δύναμις
כי	ἀλλά, εἰ(ἦ) μήν, ὅτι
כל	πᾶς
כלה	νύμφη
כלי	σκεῦος
<u>כליון</u>	ἐκλείπω
כסף	ἀργύριον, ἀργυροῦς
<u>כפוף</u>	κύπτων
כרת	ἵστημι
כשל	ἀσθενέω
כתב	γράφω
אל	→ -ל
לא	οὐκ
לב	καρδία, <u>ψυχή</u>
לבונה	λίβανος
לבלתי	πρὸς τὸ μή
לזועה/לזעוה	ὑποχείριος, <u>ὄφλησις</u>
לילה	νύξ
לכד	λαμβάνω
למטה	ὑποκάτω
(ל)מן	ἀπό
למעלה	ἐπάνω
למען	ἕνεκεν, ἵνα
לפני	ἔναντι, ἐναντίον, ἐνώπιον, κατὰ πρόσωπον
לקח	λαμβάνω
מן	ἀπό, ἐκ
מאין	ἀπό
מועד	καιρός
מועצה	(δια)νόημα
מופת	τέρας
מות	(ἀπο)θνήσκω

49

מזבח θυσιαστήριον
מחשבה (δια)νόημα
מלך βασιλεύς
ממלכה βασιλεία
מן ἀπό, ἐκ
מנחה μαναα
מסגר δεσμώτης
מעון οἶκος
מְעַט ὀλίγος, μικρός
מעט σμικρύνομαι
מעל ἀπό
מעללים πράγματα
מעשה ἔργον
מצא εὑρίσκω
מקום τόπος
מרד ἀπειθέω
המרה ἀπειθέω
נא δή
הביט ἐννοέω
נביא προφήτης
נגעים πόνοι
הדיח διασπείρω
נהר ποταμός
נטה κλίνω
נטוי ὑψηλός
הפיל καταβάλλω
נפש ψυχή
הציל ἐξαιρέω
השיג δύναμαι
נתן δίδωμι, τίθημι
נתש κινέω
סביב κύκλῳ
סור σχεδιάζω
ספר βιβλίον, βίβλος
עֶבֶד παῖς
עבד δουλεύω, ἐργάζομαι
עַד ἕως
עֹד αἰών
עוד ἔτι
עוה ἀσεβέω
עולם αἰώνιος
עון ἀδικία
עז ἰσχύς

עָטוּף ἀκηδιῶν
עין ὀφθαλμός ; → בעיני
עיר πόλις
על ἐπί ; → מעל
על כן διὰ τοῦτο
עולה ὁλοκαύτωμα
העלה ἀναφέρω
עם εἰς, μετά, πρός
עם γένος, λαός
עצם ὀστοῦν
ערף νῶτον
עשה ποιέω
עשרה δέκατος
עת καιρός
עתה νῦν
התפלל (προσ)εύχομαι
פנים πρόσωπον, πρόσωπα ; → לפני
פקח ἀνοίγνυμι
פשע ἀφίστημι
צבאות (ה׳) (κύριος) παντοκράτωρ
צדיק δίκαιος
צדקה δικαιοσύνη, δικαίωμα
צואר ὦμος
צוה ἐντέλλομαι, συντάσσω
צום νηστεύω
צל σκιά
צעק κράζω
צרה στενά
קבץ συνάγω
קדש ἅγιος
קול φωνή
הקים ἵστημι
קטן μικρός
קרא ἀναγιγνώσκω, ἐπικαλέω, κράζω
קרח παγετός
קשב ἀκούω
קשה/קשי σκληρός
קשה ערף σκληροτράχηλος
ראה ὁράω
רב μέγας, πολύς
הרבה πληθύνω
רגז λυπέομαι
רגל → גדל
רוח πνεῦμα

רחמים	οἰκτιρμός
רַע, רָע	κακός, πονηρός
רעב	λιμός
רעה	τὰ κακά, πονηρία
רשע	ἀδικέω
שאול	ᾅδης
נשאר	καταλείπομαι
שבה	ἀποικίζω
שבי	ἀποικία, ἀποικισμός
נשבע	ὄμνυμι
שבעה	ἑβδόμη
השבית	ἔκλειψιν ποιέω
שוב	ἀποστρέφω, ἐπιστρέφω
שים לב	ἐννοέω
שכן	κάθημαι
שלח	ἀποστέλλω, ἐνίημι
השליך	ἐκρίπτομαι
שֵׁם	ὄνομα
שָׁם	ἐκεῖ
שמה, שממה	ἄβατος; ἔρημος
שמחה	χαρμονή, χαρμοσύνη
שמים	οὐρανός
שמע	ἀκούω, εἰσακούω, ὑπακούω
שנה	ἔτος
שֹׁפֵט	δικαστής
שפט	δικάζω
שקד	γρηγορέω
השקיף	καθοράω
שר	ἄρχων
שרף	ἐμπίπρημι
שררות	διάνοια
שָׂשׂוֹן	εὐφροσύνη
תורה	νόμος, πρόσταγμα
תחלאים	πόνοι
תחנונים	δέησις
תחת	ὑποκάτω
תפלה	προσευχή

51